First World War
and Army of Occupation
War Diary
France, Belgium and Germany

39 DIVISION
Headquarters, Branches and Services
Royal Army Ordnance Corps
Deputy Assistant Director Ordnance Services
26 February 1916 - 28 February 1919

WO95/2573/2

The Naval & Military Press Ltd
www.nmarchive.com
Published in association with The National Archives

Published by

The Naval & Military Press Ltd

Unit 10 Ridgewood Industrial Park,

Uckfield, East Sussex,

TN22 5QE England

Tel: +44 (0) 1825 749494

www.naval-military-press.com

www.nmarchive.com

This diary has been reprinted in facsimile from the original. Any imperfections are inevitably reproduced and the quality may fall short of modern type and cartographic standards.

© **Crown Copyright**
Images reproduced by permission of The National Archives, London, England, 2015.

Contents

Document type	Place/Title	Date From	Date To
Heading	WO95/2573/2		
Heading	39th Division D.A. Dir. Ordnance Services Feb 1916-Feb 1919		
War Diary	St. Omer	26/02/1916	26/02/1916
War Diary	Amettes	27/02/1916	28/02/1916
War Diary	Boeseghem	29/02/1916	29/02/1916
War Diary	Blaringhem	01/03/1916	24/03/1916
War Diary	Lestrem	25/03/1916	15/04/1916
War Diary	Locon	16/04/1916	31/05/1916
War Diary	Officer i/c A. G's Office Base	01/07/1916	01/07/1916
War Diary	Locon	01/06/1916	07/07/1916
War Diary	Bethune	08/07/1916	14/07/1916
War Diary	Locon	15/07/1916	11/08/1916
War Diary	Roellecourt	12/08/1916	23/08/1916
War Diary	Bus-Les-Artois	24/08/1916	31/08/1916
War Diary	Acheux	01/09/1916	05/10/1916
War Diary	Hodauville Warloy Rd	06/10/1916	06/10/1916
War Diary	V.9.a.4.5. Sheet 57D	07/10/1916	14/11/1916
War Diary	V.9.a.4.5	15/11/1916	16/11/1916
War Diary	Hazebrouck	17/11/1916	17/11/1916
War Diary	Esquelbecq	18/11/1916	13/12/1916
War Diary	Poperinghe	14/12/1916	16/02/1917
War Diary	Esquelbecq	17/02/1917	27/02/1917
War Diary	G.14.b.6.4 Sheet 28	28/02/1917	31/03/1917
War Diary	G14b.6.4	01/04/1917	09/04/1917
War Diary	Poperinge	10/04/1917	31/05/1917
War Diary	Sheet 28 A.22.d.5.3	01/06/1917	06/08/1917
War Diary	Meteren	07/08/1917	14/08/1917
War Diary	Westoutre	15/08/1917	11/10/1917
War Diary	Dezon Camp Sheet 28 M.18. A.4.9	12/10/1917	23/10/1917
War Diary	De Zon Camp	24/10/1917	24/10/1917
War Diary	Reninghelst	25/10/1917	27/10/1917
War Diary	St. Jans Capell	28/10/1917	31/10/1917
War Diary	St. Jans Capel	01/10/1917	25/10/1917
War Diary	De Zon Camp Sheet 28 M.18.a.4.9	26/10/1917	31/10/1917
War Diary	De Zon Camp M.18a.4.9	01/11/1917	15/11/1917
War Diary	Westoutre	16/11/1917	26/11/1917
War Diary	Steenvoorde	17/11/1917	08/12/1917
War Diary	Neilles Lez Blequin	09/12/1917	26/12/1917
War Diary	A.23.d.5.3 Sheet 28	01/01/1918	21/01/1918
War Diary	Amiens	22/01/1918	23/01/1918
War Diary	Mericourt Sur. Somme	24/01/1918	30/01/1918
War Diary	Nurlu	01/02/1918	12/03/1918
War Diary	Haut Allaines	13/03/1918	22/03/1918
War Diary	Maricourt	23/03/1918	23/03/1918
War Diary	Chuignes-Bray-Proyart Road.	24/03/1918	25/03/1918
War Diary	Hamelette	26/03/1918	26/03/1918
War Diary	Boves	27/03/1918	30/03/1918
War Diary	St Fuscien	31/03/1918	31/03/1918
War Diary	Guignemicourt	01/04/1918	02/04/1918

War Diary	Oisemont	03/04/1918	05/04/1918
War Diary	Calais	06/04/1918	06/04/1918
War Diary	Watten	07/04/1918	14/08/1918
War Diary	Watten	01/08/1918	15/08/1918
War Diary	Dieppe	16/08/1918	16/08/1918
War Diary	Varengeville	17/08/1918	31/08/1918
War Diary	Watten	15/08/1918	15/08/1918
War Diary	Dieppe	16/08/1918	16/08/1918
War Diary	Varengeville	17/08/1918	26/08/1918
War Diary	Varengeville	01/10/1918	28/02/1919

W095/25731/2

39TH DIVISION

D. A. DIR. ORDNANCE SERVICES

~~MAR~~ FEB 1916 - FEB 1919

39TH DIVISION

Army Form C. 2118

WAR DIARY
— or —
INTELLIGENCE SUMMARY
(Erase heading not required.)

Instructions regarding War Diaries and Intelligence Summaries are contained in F. S. Regs., Part II. and the Staff Manual respectively. Title Pages will be prepared in manuscript.

Place	Date	Hour	Summary of Events and Information	Remarks and references to Appendices
ST. OMER	26.2.16	11-0 p.m.	Arrived here from England via BOULOGNE with Advance Party of Headquarters Staff 39th Division. Sleeping here tonight.	
AMETTES	27.2.16	10-0 p.m.	Motored here from ST OMER, arriving in afternoon.	
"	28.2.16	10-0 p.m.	Selected site for Divisional Dumps and assisted in Billeting arrangements.	
BOESEGHEM	29.2.16	10-0 p.m.	Arrived here after proceeding to BLARINGHEM to take over area of 23rd Division in III Corps area 1st Army.	

B.P. Smith Lieut
ADVS 39th Division

1875 Wt. W 593/826 1,000,000 4/15 J.B.C. & A. A.D.S.S./Forms/C. 2118.

Army Form C. 2118

WAR DIARY
or
INTELLIGENCE SUMMARY
(Erase heading not required.)

Instructions regarding War Diaries and Intelligence Summaries are contained in F.S. Regs., Part II. and the Staff Manual respectively. Title Pages will be prepared in manuscript.

Place	Date	Hour	Summary of Events and Information	Remarks and references to Appendices
BLARINGHEM	1.3.16	10-0 p.m.	Made arrangements for supply of Ordnance Stores to Divisions and attended sale for Ordnance Dumps - the Sheets hung at a point on Sheet 36A 40.000 Dig A.3.2. (MORBECQUE).	[R]
"	2.3.16	10-0 p.m.	Made arrangements for Divisional Armourers Shops from found suitable workshops opposite Dumps.	[R]
"	3.3.16	10-0 p.m.	Visited A.D.O.S. III Corps and discussed matters affecting supply to the Divisions.	[R]
"	4.3.16	10-0 p.m.	Attending to office routine and from up my office in BLARINGHEM.	[R]
"	5.3.16	10-0 p.m.	Attended Conference at office of A.D.O.S. III Corps and subsequently visited D.A.D.O.S. 24th Division and T.O.M. No 22 workshops.	[R]
"	6.3.16	10-0 p.m.	Attending to routine office work	[R]
"	7.3.16	10-0 p.m.	Met Chief Clerk and part of Staff at BLARINGHEM on arrival from England. Instructed them in the supply of Ordnance Stores in the field.	[R]
"	8.3.16	10-0 p.m.	Visited Dumps and attended to office work. Visited D.D.O.S. 1st Army and R.T.O. AIRE.	[R]
"	9.3.16	10-0 p.m.	Visited Dumps and T.O.M. No 22 Workshops made arrangements for the repair of Vehicles of the Division.	[R]
"	10.3.16	10-0 p.m.	Visited Dumps and Supervised the issue of Ordnance Stores. Attended to office work	[R]

WAR DIARY or INTELLIGENCE SUMMARY

(Erase heading not required.)

Army Form C. 2118

Instructions regarding War Diaries and Intelligence Summaries are contained in F.S. Regs., Part II. and the Staff Manual respectively. Title Pages will be prepared in manuscript.

Place	Date	Hour	Summary of Events and Information	Remarks and references to Appendices
BLARINGHEM	11.3.16	10-0 p.m.	Visited Dumps and Railhead. Supervised issue of stores and attended to office routine.	DA1
"	12.3.16	10-0 p.m.	Attended Conference at office of D.A.D.O.S. VII Corps and came back to Dump.	DA1
"	13.3.16	10-0 p.m.	Visited Dump, Railhead and attended to office routine.	DA1
"	14.3.16	10-0 p.m.	Visited Dump and Railhead. P.M. he is Workshop.	DA1
"	15.3.16	10-0 p.m.	Visited D.D.O.S. 1st Army. Attended to Office routine & general supervision of issues.	DA1
"	16.3.16	10-0 p.m.	Visited Dump and supervised issues.	DA1
"	17.3.16	10-0 p.m.	Visited Dump and accompanied A.D.O.S. VII Corps.	DA1
"	18.3.16	10-0 p.m.	Supervised work in Armourers Shops and Dump.	DA1
"	19.3.16	10-0 p.m.	Attended Conference at Office of D.A.D.O.S. VII Corps & supervised office and work in Dump.	DA1
"	20.3.16	10-0 p.m.	Visited Dumps and attended to office routine.	DA1
"	21.3.16	10-0 p.m.	Visited units and Dump.	DA1
"	22.3.16	10-0 p.m.	Visited Railhead and attended to Office work.	DA1
"	23.3.16	10-0 p.m.	Visited Dumps and supervised disposal of stores & etc.	DA1
"	24.3.16	10-0 p.m.	Visited ST VENANT to select Ordnance Dumps the divisions being attached to XI Corps area. Found convenient place and gave instruction for removal of my stores.	DA1
LESTREM	25.3.16	10-0 p.m.	Removed stores from MORBECQUE and established office at ST VENANT and during hrs here billets.	DA1
"	26.3.16	10-0 p.m.	Visited Dumps, supervised issue of stores and attended to office routine amongst this latter.	DA1

1875 Wt. W593/826 1,000,000 4/15 J.B.C. & A. A.D.S.S./Forms/C. 2118.

Army Form C. 2118

WAR DIARY
INTELLIGENCE SUMMARY
(Erase heading not required.)

Instructions regarding War Diaries and Intelligence Summaries are contained in F. S. Regs., Part II. and the Staff Manual respectively. Title Pages will be prepared in manuscript.

Place	Date	Hour	Summary of Events and Information	Remarks and references to Appendices
LESTREM	27.3.16	11-8pm	Visited dumps and experience dispatch of stores to units temporarily attached to the Division	AD/
	28.3.16	11-6pm	Attended to office routine & experienced work in Camps	AD/
	29.3.16	11-3pm	Visited units and attended to work of office.	AD/
	30.3.16	11-7pm	Large amount of Ordnance arriving and experience issue of same	AD/
	31.3.16	11-6pm	Attended to office routine and matters of Ord. to 17 workshops.	AD/

D.R.Smith Capt.
D.A.D.O.S. 39 t Division

DADOS
39 Div Vol 2

WAR DIARY or INTELLIGENCE SUMMARY

(Erase heading not required.)

Army Form C. 2118

Place	Date	Hour	Summary of Events and Information	Remarks and references to Appendices
LESTREM	1.4.16	11.0 p.m.	Visited Dumps & Supervised issues and worked until - attended to office work.	BE/
"	2.4.16	11.0 p.m.	Attended to office routine and Supervised issues	BE/
"	3.4.16	11.0 p.m.	Attended to office routine. Visited Railhead MERVILLE and Dumps	BE/
"	4.4.16	11.0 p.m.	Attended to office routine. General supervision of issues and visited Railhead	BE/
"	5.4.16	11.0 p.m.	Supervised issue of stores and attended to office work.	BE/
"	6.4.16	11.0 p.m.	Visited Railhead and attended to issue of stores and office work.	BE/
"	7.4.16	11.0 p.m.	Visited A.D.O.S. XI Corps HINGES and attended to office work.	BE/
"	8.4.16	11.0 p.m.	Visited 117 Infantry Brigade Headquarters and Supervised issue of stores	BE/
"	9.4.16	11.0 p.m.	Visited Headquarters 39 Art. 12 A and attended to office work	BE/
"	10.4.16	11.0 p.m.	Visited Railhead. D.A.D.O.S. 38 Division	BE/
"	11.4.16	11.0 p.m.	Visited unit of 116 Infantry Brigade and attended to office work	BE/
"	12.4.16	11.0 p.m.	Attended to office work. Also supervised issue of stores	BE/
"	13.4.16	11.0 p.m.	Visited D.A.D.O.S 38 Division and attending to office work.	BE/
"	14.4.16	11.0 p.m.	Visited Railhead and attended to office work.	BE/
"	15.4.16	11.0 p.m.	Visited DADOS 38 Division and made arrangements to take over Dumps from him.	BE/
LOCON	16.4.16	10.0 p.m.	The Division having moved into this area occupied by 38 Division, LOCON was now established by the Headquarters 39 Division and all of Ordnance Dumps. Between stores and new farm ST VENANT has only one Lorries two of which were at refilling points. Adopted the system of sending stores to Refilling points A.S.C.	BE/
"	17.4.16	10.0 p.m.	Attending to office work and arranging Dumps	BE/
"	18.4.16	10.0 p.m.	Visited Railway LA GORGUE additional flag Refilling points Refilling system working excellently and the scheme to this is greatly facilitated the consignee stores are not of Bell copying about the Dumps.	BE/

Army Form C. 2118

WAR DIARY
or
INTELLIGENCE SUMMARY
(Erase heading not required.)

Place	Date	Hour	Summary of Events and Information	Remarks and references to Appendices
LOCON	19.4.16	10-0 pm	Attended to office work and dumps. Visited Railhead.	
"	20.4.16	10-0 pm	Visited Refilling points. Attended to office work. Visited units.	
"	21.4.16	10-0 pm	Visited Railhead and attended to office work.	
"	22.4.16	10-0 pm	Visited Refilling points A.D.V.S. X1 Corps attended to office work.	
"	23.4.16	10-0 pm	Visited Railhead and observed work in Corps Zone.	
"	24.4.16	10-0 pm	Attended to office work on line motor units.	
"	25.4.16	10-0 pm	Visited Refilling points and attended to office work.	
"	26.4.16	10-0 pm	Attended to work in Camp and visited A.D.V.S X1 Corps.	
"	27.4.16	10-0 pm	Visited Railhead and units.	
"	28.4.16	10-0 pm	Visited Refilling points and supervised work in camp.	
"	29.4.16	10-0 pm	Attended to office work and visited Railhead.	
"	30.4.16	10-0 pm	Visited units and attended to office work.	

J. Church Capt
D.A.D.V.S. 39 Division

WAR DIARY or INTELLIGENCE SUMMARY

Army Form C. 2118

DA 785 323

Vol 3

Place	Date	Hour	Summary of Events and Information	Remarks and references to Appendices
LOCON	1.5.16	10-0pm	Visited Railhead & personnel none of store	
"	2.5.16	10-0pm	Visited Refilling points and units. Attended to office work	
"	3.5.16	10-0pm	Visited Railhead and attended to office matters	
"	4.5.16	10-0pm	Attended Refilling points – Visited units and A.D.S. & Bde	
"	5.5.16	10-0pm	Visited Railhead (and informal none of stores)	
"	6.5.16	10-0pm	Visited Refilling points and units and attended to office matters	
"	7.5.16	10-0pm	Visited Railhead – an experiment run of stores	
"	8.5.16	10-0pm	Visited Refilling points. Received 2000 P.H. Helmets for Divisional Reserve	
"	9.5.16	10-0pm	Visited Railhead and attended to office matters	
"	10.5.16	10-0pm	Attended refilling points. Informal none of stores in Dumps	
"	11.5.16	10-0pm	Visited units (a 45th (Div)) Conformed her "Kys" A/186 Bde. Remarks as in explanation.	
"	12.5.16	10-0pm	Visited Refilling points and attended to office matters	
"	13.5.16	10-0pm	Visited Railhead and units	
"	14.5.16	10-0pm	Constant to office work and issue of stores from Dump	
"	15.5.16	10-0pm	Visited A.O.D. & Bde & DADOS of 38th Division	
"	16.5.16	10-0pm	Visited Refilling points and units	
"	17.5.16	10-0pm	Attended to office matters	
"	18.5.16	10-0pm	Visited Railhead (and informal none of stores)	
"	19.5.16	10-0pm	Visited Refilling points and units	
"	20.5.16	10-0pm	Attended to office work and issue of stores from Dumps	
"	21.5.16	10-0pm	Visited Refilling points and attended to office work	
"	22.5.16	10-0pm	Observed issue of stores at Dumps and visited units	

Army Form C. 2118

WAR DIARY
or
INTELLIGENCE SUMMARY
(Erase heading not required.)

Instructions regarding War Diaries and Intelligence Summaries are contained in F. S. Regs., Part II. and the Staff Manual respectively. Title Pages will be prepared in manuscript.

Place	Date	Hour	Summary of Events and Information	Remarks and references to Appendices
LOCON	23.5.16	10.0pm	Visited Caithorn and experiment room of stores from Refilling point.	
"	24.5.16	10.0pm	Attended to office work.	
"	25.5.16	10.0pm	Visited A.S.C. xy Corps and issues.	
"	26.5.16	10.0pm	Afternoon issue of stores at Refilling point	
"	27.5.16	10.0pm	Attended to office work	
"	28.5.16	10.0pm	Visited Refilling point and arranged to work in Boots	
"	29.5.16	10.0pm	Visited Refilling point and issues	
"	30.5.16	10.0pm	Attended to office work	
"	31.5.16	10.0pm	Visited Caithorn and attended to office routine	

S.O.Smith Capt
S.S.O. 29 Division

11/18

Secret

Officer i/c
A. G's Office
Base

[stamp: D.A.D.O.S. 39th DIVISION No.......... 1- JUL 1916]

I herewith enclose my War Diary for the Month of June 1916.

Will you please acknowledge receipt hereon.

[signature]
Capt.
DADOS 39th Dⁿ

1/7/16.

WAR DIARY or INTELLIGENCE SUMMARY

Army Form C. 2118

Vol 4 June
39. D.A.D.O.S

Place	Date	Hour	Summary of Events and Information	Remarks and references to Appendices
LOCON	1.6.16	10-6pm	Visited Refilling Points and returned one of Armd. Temp Lt Shultern arrived for duty A.O.D.	BPI
"	2.6.16	10-6pm	Visited Coulhel and unit	BPI
"	3.6.16	10-6pm	Visited Refilling Points A.O.D. X1 Corps	BPI
"	4.5.16	10-6pm	Visited Refilling Points and returned to office routine	BPI
"	6.6.16	8.0 am	Visited camp and left for England on leave. Temp Lt Shultern is acting in my absence	
"	16.6.16	10-6pm	Arrived from England and took over from Lieut Shultern	BPI
"	17.8.16	10-6pm	Visited Coulhele began to see if it was practicable to back up the stores at Coulhele and distribute to the fore lines. For this purpose I am going to visit at Refilling Points the same day. This afternoon four motor lorries will for the five lorries	BPI
"	18.6.16	10-6pm	Visited Ranchard 6.0 am and afterwards assembly stores to four lorries. The operation will start No less are the stores here delivered to the unit without difficulty. The refilling points are on the same road and the distance from the Coulhele to all refilling point is about 5 miles. This is a very good system of supply allowing to unit about twenty any stores are lying about all the dumps Marked Coulhele and independance distribution of stores to firms. Visited units in the Division are A.O.D. X1 Corps.	BPI
"	19.6.16	10-6pm	Visited Refilling and unit in the office all day	BPI
"	20.6.16	10-6pm	Visited Refilling and unit of the Div. Temp Lt Shultern left for duty with 2nd Army	BPI
"	21.6.16	10-6pm	Visited Coulhele and units of Division	BPI
"	22.6.16	10-6pm	Visited Refilling and units of Division	BPI
"	23.6.16	10-6pm	Visited Refilling Points	BPI
"	24.6.16	10-6pm	Visited Coulhele Ramena of Grenade more. There has been getting out arrangements for supply.	BPI
"	25.6.16	10-6pm	Visited Coulhele Distribution scheme working perfectly	BPI

Army Form C. 2118

WAR DIARY
INTELLIGENCE SUMMARY
(Erase heading not required.)

Instructions regarding War Diaries and Intelligence Summaries are contained in F. S. Regs., Part II. and the Staff Manual respectively. Title Pages will be prepared in manuscript.

Place	Date	Hour	Summary of Events and Information	Remarks and references to Appendices
LOCON	26.6.16	10-0pm	Visited Rush hut and adults of stores into Bel Croix. Various units of Division	
	27.6.16	10-0pm	Division to be equipped with (Lewis Guns for keeping wid. at present in possession of it for anti	
	28.6.16		aircraft hay to complete to this scale.	
	29.6.16	10-0pm	Visited Rush hut nothing to return work.	
	30.6.16	10-0pm		

A. Rhuch Lyst A.O.D.
D.A.D.O.S. 39th Division

1875 Wt. W593/826 1,000,000 4/15 J.B.C. & A. A.D.S.S./Forms/C. 2118.

WAR DIARY
or
INTELLIGENCE SUMMARY
(Erase heading not required.)

Army Form C. 2118

July Vol 5
DADOS
89 Div

Place	Date	Hour	Summary of Events and Information	Remarks and references to Appendices
LOCON	1.7.16	11-0pm	Another Raidhead and alongwith refilling point. Two Lewis Guns demanded from here to replace two lost by 13 Rifle Brigade	BM
"	2.7.16	10-0pm	Visited Refr R Supply Points. Three Lewis Guns demanded from Base to replace three lost in the above mentioned raid. Received 26 Lewis Guns. The	BM
"	3.7.16	10-0pm	Equipt the Division to 6 per Infantry unit. Demanded 1·3" Stokes Mortar to replace recently Visited R.R. Exchange	BM
"	4.7.16	10-0pm	Received 5 Lewis Guns and 3" Stokes Mortar flammanure. Quick to anti- concussion Visited to Refill and if the Pioneers were in a forward or rearward role. Gave the deputy pioneers to the Brigade Lewis (+) at Railhead. Know the new home of my Clerk, Clk and 4 Storemen. The Lewis provision of Refilling Point and were met by B.M. & MO who landed on the representation of the units as they passed with rations. System worked extremely well.	BM
"	5.7.16	10-0pm	Detrailhead stores at Railhead and worked on the same system. The Refilling point being altered by D.H.Q. in the afternoon of 4th. Visited Bdl headquarters. The 14/13 Green (two units of this Brigade) lost in considerable amount of stores, but these have practically met all demands.	BM
"	6.7.16	10-0pm	Visited Refilling Point.	BM
"	7.7.16	10-0pm	Visited Railhead Refilling Point. Demands made other to move to BETHUNE	BM
BETHUNE	8.7.16	10-0pm	Visited Railhead Refilling Point. All stores issued - Moved to Bethune to rejoin 33a Division	BM
BETHUNE	9.7.16	10-0pm	Detrailhead stores at Railhead cleared Dumps, Armourers' Whp, Bootmakers Whp and Pioneers Whp. All shops working	BM

WAR DIARY
or
INTELLIGENCE SUMMARY
(Erase heading not required.)

Army Form C. 2118

Place	Date	Hour	Summary of Events and Information	Remarks and references to Appendices
BETHUNE	10.7.16	11-5pm	Visited Railhead and distributed stores to Brigade lorries. Daily routine work	
	11.7.16	11-2pm	do	
	12.7.16	11-5pm	do	
	13.7.16	11-5pm	do	
	14.7.16	11-5pm	do	
	15.7.16	11-5pm	do	
LOCON	16.7.16	11-5pm	Visited Railhead and refilling point. The Division Headquarters return again to LOCON. Moved all shops stamp today and offices working by 12.30 hour.	
	17.7.16	11-5pm	Visited Railhead & Refilling points	
	18.7.16	11-5pm	do	
	19.7.16	11-5pm	do	
	20.7.16	11-5pm	do	
	21.7.16	11-5pm		
	22.7.16	11-5pm	Visited Refilling points & units of 1st Division	
	23.7.16	11-5pm	do	
	24.7.16	11-5pm	Visited Railhead and attended to Daily routine work	
	25.7.16	11-5pm	do	
	26.7.16	11-5pm	do	
	27.7.16	11-5pm	do	
	28.7.16	11-5pm	Visited Refilling points and units	
	29.7.16	11-5pm	Visited Railhead in reference to daily Routine work	
	30.7.16	11-5pm	Visited Railhead units	
	31.7.16	11-5pm	Visited Refilling points and Routine work	

1.8.16

B.R. Smith Capt
D.A.D.O.S. 29 Div

SECRET

WAR DIARY of ADS 39 Div

INTELLIGENCE SUMMARY

Vol 6 — Page 1

Army Form C. 2118

(Erase heading not required.)

Instructions regarding War Diaries and Intelligence Summaries are contained in F.S. Regs., Part II. and the Staff Manual respectively. Title Pages will be prepared in manuscript.

Place	Date	Hour	Summary of Events and Information	Remarks and references to Appendices
LOCON	1.8.16	10.30pm	Visited Eulhead and Refilling Points. Refilling points are again never to there own to supplying to outlying units	
"	2.8.16	10.30pm	Visited Refilling Points and Railhead	
"	3.8.16	10.30pm	Visited Railhead and Refilling Points	
"	4.8.16	10.30pm	Visited Refilling Points Railhead	
"	5.8.16	10.30pm	do	
"	6.8.16	"	do	
"	7.8.16	"	do	
"	8.8.16	"	do	
"	9.8.16	"	do	
"	10.8.16	"	do	
"	11.8.16	"	do	
ROELLECOURT	12.8.16		Headquarters Division moved to ROELLECOURT and came under XVII Corps 3rd Army. The Ordnance Stores here delivered to Refilling Points as usual. Three Refilling Points are situated many miles apart and three are 15 miles from Railhead (VILLERS) Unit still along with ROELLECOURT area are an Refilling Points are again attacked and also then for refilling. Railhead still VILLERS	
"	13.8.16		This involves long hrs by the units and supplies are at an but necessary to [task?] the here to outspread roams. Reported to ADM XVIIE Corps. Visited Expedne TINCQUES and Refilling Points- also unit by of the brie much experience great difficulties they meet the supply of stores to the unit.	
"	14.8.16		Visited Railhead & Refilling Points. am making a systematic road to each unit Examining by G.R. Stores left.	

WAR DIARY or INTELLIGENCE SUMMARY

Army Form C. 2118

Page 2

Place	Date	Hour	Summary of Events and Information	Remarks and references to Appendices
ROELLECOURT	16.5.16	11.0pm	Visited Railhead and units	
"	17.5.16	11.0pm	Visited Railhead and units. No complaints. Everything in order.	
"	18.5.16	11.0pm	do	
"	19.5.16	11.0pm	do	
"	20.5.16	11.0pm	do	
"	21.5.16	11.0pm	Visited Railhead & units. The Artillery are now with Reserve Army. Am making arrangements to supply & refilling point on the line of march.	
"	22.5.16	11.0pm	Artillery Refilling Point a great advantage. Visited the Railhead Park. Rail workshops best always in working order. Everything in working order.	
"	23.5.16	11.0pm	Moved to new area do ACHEUX.	
BUS-LES-ARTOIS	24.5.16	11.0pm	Division moves to this area and came under V. Corps Reserve. Army Railhead Doullens 220 Siding 1 train.	
BUS-LES-ARTOIS	25.5.16	11.0pm	Received & issued 26 Lorries Corps to complete Div. to 8 feet trail.	
"	26.5.16	10.0pm	Motor Lorry Railhead (BOUQUEMAISON) This now Railhead. Visited new Railhead BELLE EGLISE. Very refilling parade. Timing Good.	
"	27.5.16	11.0pm	Cuts and received a great quantity of stores. Headquarters & ammunition moved to ACHEUX. Stores delivered to Refilling points as usual. 29 th Div bullock & baggage too . a Mount. Militia.	
"	28.5.16	11.0pm	Refilling Point's changed. Visited Railhead. Timing	
"	29.5.16	11.0pm	No change at Refilling Point. O Good but have horseline effected too.	
"	30.5.16	6.0pm	Visited B/gs Railhead & Refilling Points.	
"	31.5.16	11.0pm	do	

B.P.Christi Capt. A.O.D
D.A.D.O.S 39 Div.

WAR DIARY of Capt. R. Chick.

~~INTELLIGENCE SUMMARY~~ RMO 29 Div.

Army Form C. 2118

Vol 7

(Erase heading not required.)

Place	Date	Hour	Summary of Events and Information	Remarks and references to Appendices
ACHEUX	1.9.16	10.0 a.m.	Visited ADS of 87 Bde - Railhead Refilling point.	
	2.9.16	10.30 a.m.	Visited Railhead Refilling point. Ordered 67 18pr cartouches for forwards. The Division is preparing to attack on a large scale. All units equipped with steel helmets and each man in is equipped to carry 2 days of magazines.	
	3.9.16	10-4 pm	Visited Railhead Refilling point. Division made the attack but neither met success — got into boche wire both the Divisional Salvage Officer and ended — the advance salvage dumps. This was established at the Advanced Aid Post ENGLEBELMER and arrangements to collect all ordnance stores and sent a lorry to fetch them up. Will care the cooks and 1 unarmed runner each and the remainder to Railhead, Ordered 67 18pr arrived at Railhead.	
	4.9.16	10 pm	Visited Railhead Refilling points. Wanted advance salvage dumps and the Lewis Guns collected and this will be brought to a Good many Lewis Guns have been lost 6 Lewis + 2 Vickers were recovered try to replace them lost and everything by Skill Fire — Was able to Re-equip the 2 Brigades with 1133 Steel Helmets — 900 of these were obtained from L Wage Visited Brigades to ascertain what was returned from the Field Railhead Refilling Points.	
	5.9.16	10-4 pm, 6 pm-10 pm		
	6.9.16	a.m.	Visited advanced Salvage dump. Ordered Refilling point. 9 Lewis Guns, 3 Vickers & 2 ? Trench sent ours — arranged to refused others but never had to.	

WAR DIARY or INTELLIGENCE SUMMARY

Army Form C. 2118

Place	Date	Hour	Summary of Events and Information	Remarks and references to Appendices
ACHEUX	7.9.16	11.0 pm	8 Lieut. B Picton and Pte. Moss had returned to unit at Rpllsing Point. 1 Lieut. & 3 O.R. Motors evacuated to officers' hos. and destroyed by ODS fire. Visited Rpllsing Point. Salvage still being collected of my lorry. 300 Rifles collected. Visited Atd. Reg. Pt for P.O. 25th.	App
	8.9.16	9pm	9 Others + 2 Trench Mortars received evacuation to units at Rpllsing Point. Worked Field Ambulance & equipment taken from evacuated men.	App
	9.9.16	9pm	1 Lieut. – 3 Others – 3 Stokes Mortars arrived from here and issued to units at Rpllsing Point. During the equipment with regard to armament and retrieval of Stokes Mortars that had been a great deal of pearl of Stokes Mortars. No portholes (without? is cemented in Rpllsing Point. The portholes (without? is cemented to use counter)	App
	10.9.16	11.0 pm	Visited Rallied Rpllsing Point. Have put men on to sort out salvage of find that others are away from here, clearly for replacement	App
	11.9.16	11 pm	Visited Rallied Rpllsing Point are units.	App
	12.9.16	11.0 pm	Visited Rallied Rpllsing Point and ADS 2 C/Rs.	App
	13.9.16	1-3pm	Visited Rallied Rpllsing Point. Salvage dumps visits	App
	14.9.16	1-3pm	do	App
	15.9.16	1-3pm	do	App
	16.9.16	1-3pm	do	App
	17.9.16	1 pm	Visited ADS & 6 C/Rs Rpllsing Point have put here to write demand for 1st Hants Regt.	App
	18.9.16		Visited Rallied at Rpllsing Point in Kirkman P. 15/9/16.	App
	19.9.16		Visited Rallied at Rpllsing Point	App

WAR DIARY
or
INTELLIGENCE SUMMARY
(Erase heading not required.)

Army Form C. 2118

Place	Date	Hour	Summary of Events and Information	Remarks and references to Appendices
ACHEUX	20.9.16	11-0pm	Visited Railhead Refilling Point. A good deal of salvage evacuated to here. The following was collected and fwd onward:- 1985 a/c Equipment, 291 Slgs. goatskins, 870 Rifles, 624 Bayonets, 1107 Steel Helmets, 261 Haversacks, 1000 flares and 89 line belts.	[illegible]
"	21.9.16	11-0pm	Visited Railhead Refilling Point. Visited transport of Infantry Bn. [?]	[illegible]
"	22.9.16	11-0pm	do	[illegible]
"	23.9.16	11-0pm	do	[illegible]
"	24.9.16	11-0pm	do Recd A.C.H. Supp. A.O.D. forms for ambulances	[illegible]
"	25.9.16	11-0pm	do	
"	26.9.16	11-0pm	do Field Ambers. still have few cases during this month so 3" Trench Mortar Batteries to not appear to be efficient as 16 have been evacuated owing to the natal developing a cold, a flaw was that his knife removed from his knapsack	[illegible]
"	27.9.16	11-0pm	Visited Railhead Refilling Points	[illegible]
"	28.9.16	11-0pm	Visited Refilling Point and unit	[illegible]
"	29.9.16	11-0pm	Visited Railhead Refilling Point. 17th Bde horseambulance told evacuating to the North Overture Copse.	[illegible]
"	30.9.16	9pm	Visited Railhead Refilling Point. See funds for other Motors recd from here	[illegible]

Instructions regarding War Diaries and Intelligence Summaries are contained in F.S. Regs., Part II. and the Staff Manual respectively. Title Pages will be prepared in manuscript.

WAR DIARY

or

INTELLIGENCE SUMMARY

(Erase heading not required.)

Army Form C. 2118

Vol 8

Place	Date	Hour	Summary of Events and Information	Remarks and references to Appendices
ACHEUX	1.10.16	10.4pm	Visited Railhead Refilling Points Headquarters 39 Div. Went to Thievreuille and came idle the other of Lieut. SENGIS. Wrote to move troops in mistake accommodated escort to France.	
	2.10.16	10.5pm	Rode office a few yards in some village. Room vacated by IV.D/2/5. Visited Railhead Refilling Point.	
	3.10.16	10.5pm	"	
	4.10.16	10.5pm	"	
	5.10.16	10.5pm	"	
Hedauville			Tents.	
Warloy/Rd	6.10.6.10pm		Thence to camps. Arranged to move into camps and park sheds in	
V.G. a.d.	7.10.6.10pm		Visited Railhead & Refilling Point. All stores and ete. evacuated from ACHEUX	
Shed 1 Sep	8.10.6.10pm		Visited A.D.D.S. 4th Corps. Took over of Gun half shed taken over.	
	9.10.6.10pm		to Mr. Bonnefoy to receive & Sunic. Stith?	
	10.10.6.10pm		Visited Railhead & Mamsie.	
	11.10.6.10pm		Rec'd Ration Lorries as store Visited Railhead Refilling Point. The 8th Canadian T.M. Bde & Mamsie. Worked the 1st 2 Camusgrave.	
			G.7. N.Rg. Armament	
	12.10.6 am		Visited Railhead Refilling Point. 18 Bde in the regiment sent on the property. Carried the formerly by an orderly arrived about 260 yds from Mod Repo. No witness was seen in the license before	

WAR DIARY or INTELLIGENCE SUMMARY

Army Form C. 2118

(Erase heading not required.)

Place	Date	Hour	Summary of Events and Information	Remarks and references to Appendices
V.g.a.4.5. Shot. 5.7	13/10/16	10.pm	2 tanks field A.Z. 8 for support from Beaver - Vicker Riflery. Fair lot on line Pilcher Bomb	
	14.10.16	11pm	1-3" Stokes Mortar ammun. Vicker Pulchen. Salvage Dumps	
	15.10.16	11.50pm	Evac. AC. Freight spares for Reserve Army Trops.	
	16.10.16	11pm	Visited Pulchen Riflery Point. Demand 1.45 trs. Enfilade	
	17.10.16	11pm	to demand 62 Vickers, & M.G. & Lg. brig.	
	18.10.16	11pm	no 1.45 Hrs ammun at Pulchen.	
	19.10.16	11pm	2 Vickers ammun. from 118 M/G Coy. 8 Guns (4 Lewis & Vickers) and in repair. These have still returned out are ready for issue. Visited Pulchen Point.	
	20.10.16	11pm	Visited onli. Salvage Dumps. returned 15:00 Pt. Ammo to these parts of Bat Room.	
	21.10.16	11pm	2 Lewis Guns demanded from here. 7 Tanks I wonder at thing is mic	
	22.10.16	11pm		
	23.10.16	11pm	Demand 12st Hacket for Bn. in the Pulchen	
	24.10.16	11pm		
	25.10.16	11pm	Visited Riflery Point. Pulchen	
	26.10.16	11pm	G.	
	27.10.16	11pm	to by with Brid. Muchen, ammun from here	
	28.10.16	11pm	26 Lewis Guns now Carefully unlt to send of 15th Brigan	
	29.10.16	11pm	Visited Pulchen Point	
	30.10.16	11pm	Visited Riflery Point, Panie 17 Bn R.A. Mayle for ammun	
	31.10.16	11pm	Visited Pulchen Point	

BP Maj. Gen Stars 39 Bn

Army Form C. 2118

WAR DIARY
or
INTELLIGENCE SUMMARY
(Erase heading not required.)

Instructions regarding War Diaries and Intelligence Summaries are contained in F. S. Regs., Part II. and the Staff Manual respectively. Title Pages will be prepared in manuscript.

Place	Date	Hour	Summary of Events and Information	Remarks and references to Appendices
V9.A.4.5 Sh.1 54 D				

WAR DIARY of 6/L BR.SMITH
or
INTELLIGENCE SUMMARY   D.A.D.O.S. 39 DIVISION

Army Form C. 2118

Place	Date	Hour	Summary of Events and Information	Remarks and references to Appendices
V.Q.U.S	15/11/16	11-0pm	17 the Railway movement to 118 Bde & the R.A. units relieving Headquarters by Rail. Train movement to 63rd Bde. 3 train T.M. Battery movement to 63rd Bde. The Division is preparing to move by Second Army via DOULLENS	901
	16/11/16	11-30pm	Headquarters 39 Div. down to DOULLENS. H.Q. Bde. moves to one by train with all available other crafts though to keep Army. Remainder of others including Ammunition Broncos Depots and by rail from AVELUY (Railway) all others relieved to Railhead by night the Railhead is ready detail but transition was complete when entrained at ESQUELBECQ 4 trains.	
HAZEBROUCK ESQUELBECQ	17/11/16	11-0pm	Move to ESQUELBECQ. Schulleben Party office the night at HAZEBROUCK. Bde has been. There has been opened up for ...	904
	18/11/16	11-0pm	Train has to commence supply. Div. now in XVth Corps Second Army arranging to change of the	
	19/11/16	11-0pm	17 Nth & Dely Movement & Recount Army Truck/25 for Ordnance Stores	
	20/11/16	11-0pm	Horse and equipment received from um station there relieved to	
	21/11/16	11-0pm	Railway Points.	
	22/11/16	11-0pm	Visited Railhead Points	
	23/11/16	11-0pm	Visited units & Harbors	
	24/11/16	11-0pm	A great many details are coming in as the Div. is being refitting	
	25/11/16	11-0pm		
	26/11/16	11-0pm	Visited Railhead & Refitting Points	

WAR DIARY
or
INTELLIGENCE SUMMARY

Army Form C. 2118

(Erase heading not required.)

Place	Date	Hour	Summary of Events and Information	Remarks and references to Appendices
ESQUELBECQ	17/1/16	11.0 p.m	39 Div Artillery now strengthen to one Bde are annexing to reorganize into 6 gun Batteries. Visited Richens units.	
	18/1/16	11.0 p.m	Visited Artillery Parks.	
	29/1/16	11.0 p.m	118 Bde move into the line relieving the French. Divisional ae heavy trench Mors etc visited Bde Hd.quarters.	
	31/1/16	11.0 p.m	Visited Richens Artillery Park. This has been an extremely trying month from an Ordnance point of view owing to great amount of clothing the division having twenty colapsed at times, the experience gained in the days a side ideas many to the move from XIIth Decent Army. The supply of Ammunition procure, however, what uniform.	

[signature]
BGCRA 39 Div

WAR DIARY / CAPTAIN D.R. SMITH Army Form C. 2118
or
INTELLIGENCE SUMMARY
D.A.D.O.S.
29 D.I.V. 15.1.07

Vol 10

Place	Date	Hour	Summary of Events and Information	Remarks and references to Appendices
ESQUELBECQ	1.12.16	6.10.pm	Visited 118 Bde made arrangements for Trench stores in the Bde in training on return from the French	
"	2.12.16	6.10pm	A.D.O.S 5th Corps inspected dumps & lifts	
"	3.12.16	6.10pm	11 Rifles Ammo. trench mortar ordnance. Arran'd to there Army Tprs- visited Reclam. refitting Point.	
"	4.12.16	6.10pm	Nothing of importance to record. Ordnance practically complete	
"	5.12.16	—	ack'd Bde Reparators.	
"	6.12.16	6.10pm	Visited D.A.D.O.S 38 Division to see as to taking on new arrangement for trench m ordnance, etc	
POPERINGHE	7.12.16	11.10pm	Divisional Headquarters moved to SI SIXTE and have relieved the 38 Divl D.A.D.O.S. in this turn. Arrd there orders and refitting carried out as sound Reclaim shifted from PROVEN to POPERINGHE	
"	8.12.16	11.8am	Arrang'd to commence Bm Boot Repairs shops worked Refitting Point.	
"	9.12.16	11-Spm	Visited Reclaim & Laundry.	
"	10.12.16	11-Spm	20 temp base ammun bag which complete units to be for out	
"	11.12.16	11-Spm	11 Ordnance stores from trench Army trpls	

WAR DIARY
INTELLIGENCE SUMMARY
(Erase heading not required.)

Army Form C. 2118

Instructions regarding War Diaries and Intelligence Summaries are contained in F.S. Regs., Part II. and the Staff Manual respectively. Title Pages will be prepared in manuscript.

Place	Date	Hour	Summary of Events and Information	Remarks and references to Appendices
APERINGHE	9.12.16 to 26.12.16		2 Lewis Guns arrived from "Royal Munsters". This completes Nom. 6.12.1916	
"	26.12.16		Nothing of importance to record.	
"	27.12.16 10pm	19 M.Sh.	Duty returned from Lewis Gun Course	
"	28.12.16 10pm		2 Lewis Guns turned in to W.Sh. + Duty. This completes Nom. 6.12.1916	
"	29.12.16 10pm		Am preparing to overhaul all the Lewis Guns + Machine Guns of the Division and rest the Gunners of the "Moore" Sections. Have increased the practices of the Armourer Staffs from 4 to 7.	
"	30.12.16 10pm		Lewis Guns of the "Moore" returned but not quite very much worn, but Spare parts are depleted.	
"	31.12.16 10pm		The division is too practically no equipment - very few reserves are attaching.	

B.C. Smith Capt
D.A.D.S. 39 Division

WAR DIARY of CAPTAIN D.R. SMITH

INTELLIGENCE SUMMARY
(Erase heading not required.)

Army Form C. 2118

D.A.D.o.S. 29 Div 1/1/07

Vol XI

Place	Date	Hour	Summary of Events and Information	Remarks and references to Appendices
POPERINGHE	1.1.17 to 28.1.17	2-4pm	Nothing of importance to relate. Ordinary routine work.	—
"	29.1.17	11-4pm	Run Poperinge + Lovie. Returned from leave - Found my Deputy Burnue moved to fill order & am to change to 9.2.a.s.s. Hut 28	—
"	25.1.17 to 31.1.17	11-4pm	POPERINGHE. Reviewed Artillery again reorganization so as to form Army Artillery Brigade. Ordinary routine work.	—

D. R. Smith Capt
D.A.D.o.S 39 Div

WAR DIARY of CAPTAIN D.R. SMITH Army Form C. 2118
INTELLIGENCE SUMMARY — D.A.D.O.S.
2nd DIVISION.

Vol 12

Place	Date	Hour	Summary of Events and Information	Remarks and references to Appendices
POPERINGHE	1.2.17	10-4pm	Ordinary Routine Work	TRS
"	2.2.17	"	"	TRS
"	3.2.17	"	Horse bookstalls inspected by G.O.C. who expressed approval of the general arrangement of the Bn/ghs.	TRS
"	4.2.17	"	77 Bde R.F.A. joined from 16 Div.	TRS
"	5.2.17	"	77 Bde R.F.A. transferred to 38 Div.	TRS
"	"	"	Ordinary routine work.	TRS
"	6.2.17	"	Rifling Point shelled. Rural shell falling near. No casualties amongst personnel and no damage to lorries - bottles or the day's work.	TRS
"	5.2.17	"	Ordinary Routine Work.	TRS
"	6.2.17	12.0 pm	Division moving into Reserve area. Orders written at Railhead to travel and deliver to Rifling Point — One R.P. being approximately 20 miles from Railhead. As Orders to be given up to "New Petrolium" being anticipated. These precautions necessary. The return the use of all lorries to a minimum. Arrange to are removal of Stores and reserves by light railway which was to ESQUELBECQ and from there carry stores by sea. Numb by G.S. begrs.	TRS

1875 Wt. W593/325 1,000,000 4/15 J.B.C. & A. A.D.S.S./Forms/C. 2118.

Army Form C. 2118

WAR DIARY
or
INTELLIGENCE SUMMARY
(Erase heading not required.)

Place	Date	Hour	Summary of Events and Information	Remarks and references to Appendices
ESQUELBECQ	17.5.40	2–9pm	Stores carried by means of 9 1 tonners to Cheese Market, Station, POPERINGHE, before a dump not repairable to ESQUELBECQ. The question of the clearing of stores from Rackham our the supply to unit has become exceedingly difficult. The area is by very scattered and the units limited operations. Am proposing to send Personnel to Rackham. PROVEN distribute stores from there down to A.1 wagons, carry them to various gauge railway running through the area also action them to refilling point on roads. Up to the present moment have failed to obtain sanction to run a lorry or any other M.T. vehicle which is necessary to convey Personnel to Rackham.	✓
do.	18.5.40 4.30pm		Took to Rackham kitchener. Arrangers with R.T.O. to obtain 3 x 3cwt lorries. Office established and working. Permission was obtained to use the Ord Cars to Rackham with Personnel	✓
d	19.5.40 11.30am		Left at 6.0 am in charge of Personnel. Two trucks (10 tons) cleared the stores now distinctly and moved to three units refilling at Rackhead. The remainder being sent out by light railway to R.P.'s at	✓

WAR DIARY
or
INTELLIGENCE SUMMARY
(Erase heading not required.)

Army Form C. 2118

Place	Date	Hour	Summary of Events and Information	Remarks and references to Appendices
ESQUELBECQ	23.2.17	10.30am	HERZEELE and BOLLEZEELE. The Am cannot rt ort funtionly and the apply to write on therefore maintenance arr never. There were [?] experienced at time.	
"		to 10.30pm	(And more to Rubrow + being) (Custain for money this hornes mpt had given). Have detailed to R.P.'s v generally transible	
"	26.2.17	10 pm	6 heavy motor lorries. Have "Precaution Ord."	
"	24.1.17	11.30am	Purchase move to F.Corps area 0.27th and return 23rd Annover — We have some order administration of F. Corps — Have been worked over hard what is only partially race by 23rd Div — Pilkam to see this dump my site exhibit Corps there	
"	25.2.17	11.30am	Visite um [Repelling] Point and ADS's & Corps.	
"	16.2.17	11.30am	Else personnel sheet to see dumps & others dances move for her dunp	
"	27.2.17	11.00am	Remainder of others move to her dump.	
G.H.Q.6.4 Deule's	28/2/17	11.00pm	Ahmo detailed move at Rubow- has breakfast at here The has been extremely busy and moving to HOPES and also owing to the restriction on H.T. Traffic. Ohmo were Lower work to all each the same dry a receny with to suppler of the vehicles their all be capturing m as hear	

Army Form C. 2118

WAR DIARY
or
INTELLIGENCE SUMMARY
(Erase heading not required.)

of CAPTAIN D. R. SMITH. D.A.D.D.S. 39 Div VOL/3

Instructions regarding War Diaries and Intelligence Summaries are contained in F.S. Regs., Part II. and the Staff Manual respectively. Title Pages will be prepared in manuscript.

Place	Date	Hour	Summary of Events and Information	Remarks and references to Appendices
G.14.b.b.4 Shed 28	1.5.17		Nothing of importance to report	
	2.5.17	"	"	
	3.5.17	4.30pm	Visited Butte Kennedy with a view to reorganization	22/1
	4.5.17	"	Sent corp dental officers report by D.O.R.	22/2
	5.5.17	"	Visited 1 Corp. + b ops and ADMS Dept R.A	22/3
	6.5.17	"		22/4
	8.5.17	"	Ordinary routine work.	22/5
	9.5.17	"	Conference at R.A. Headqrs. All members of the Ashby were present. No complaints with regard to Dental Service.	22/6
	14.5.17	"	Conference at 117 Bde with Major & Capptain. No complaints with regard to Dental service.	22/7
	21.5.17	"	Visited D.O.D. Round Army with regard to the fall held was a conference with the Divisional Pioneer as the chemical rubber employed is dealing with the garden.	22/8
	31.5.17	"	Visited Q.M. Clothes of 117 Bde and also OC units.	22/9
			D.R. Smith Capt A.D.D.S. 39 Div	

WAR DIARY
or
INTELLIGENCE SUMMARY

(Erase heading not required.)

Army Form C. 2118

DADOS 39 D

J.S.14

Instructions regarding War Diaries and Intelligence Summaries are contained in F. S. Regs., Part II. and the Staff Manual respectively. Title Pages will be prepared in manuscript.

Place	Date	Hour	Summary of Events and Information	Remarks and references to Appendices
G14 b.6.4	1.4.17	10 pm	Nothing of importance to record - ordinary routine work. Visited mule and refilling points.	WMS
	8.4.17	10 p.m.		WMS
POPERINGHE	10.4.17	6.pm	Moved down to POPERINGHE. Division being relieved by 23rd Div. Brigade Groups thereafter all working Q.M.G. Shire	WMS
	14.4.17	6 pm	Ordinary routine work - Visited mule and refilling points.	WMS
	26.4.17	4 pm	Routine work.	WMS
	27.4.17	4 pm	Local purchases attended to.	WMS
	28.4.17	4 pm	DHQ transferred to D Camp	WMS
	30.4.17			

W. James Twiss
Major
DADOS 39th Division

D.A.D.O.S.
19 MAY 1917
39th DIVISION

WAR DIARY
INTELLIGENCE SUMMARY
(Erase heading not required.)

Army Form C. 2118

2/Capt D.R. SMITH
D.A.D.O.S. 39 DIV.

Place	Date	Hour	Summary of Events and Information	Remarks and references to Appendices
POPERINGHE	1.5.17	4 p.m.	Routine work. Purchase at BAILLEUL. Orders published for return 39 Division Artillery	
	2.5.17	4 p.m.	Markets Conference A.D.O.S. 2nd Army	
	3.5.17 to 8.5.17	4 p.m.	Routine work. Winter clothing coming in satisfactorily	
	9.5.17 to 10.5.17		Collected tent from Labour Coys - marquees & sable kitchens. Routine work	
	11.5.17		Moved Office to Nissen hut & building to hold horse for 133 Field Ambulance. Erected store tent.	
	12.5.17			
	13.5.17 to 14.5.17		Routine work. Store tent erected to replace store at Rue BOESCHEPE. Inspected Corps Dump & store rooms at Rue TÊTE D'OR in view of removal to new quarters - neither suitable. Suggested to Town Major 103 3 Division which is not in their own area.	
	15.5.17 16.5.17		Routine work.	
			Routine work.	
	17.5.17 to 21.5.17		Routine work. Town fully clothed. Am sending dumps at once. Suggested dumps at Rue Tête D'Or adopted by Chief hay. B.G.R.A. 39 Div. Office of Ordnance Stores 2nd Army. DADOS 39 Div	✓

WAR DIARY of CAPT. D R SMITH

Army Form C. 2118

D.A.D.O.S. 39 Division

INTELLIGENCE SUMMARY
(Erase heading not required.)

Vol 16

Place	Date	Hour	Summary of Events and Information	Remarks and references to Appendices
39 D.S. A.D.D.S.3	1.6.17	10-30pm	Moved office and dumps to point indicated covering temporary workshops.	ppl
	2.6.17	11-0pm	Store for return of under clothing still remain at old dump. Workshops move to new dumps.	ppl
	3.6.17	11-0pm	Visited Railhead and Refilling Point	ppl
	4.6.17	11-0pm	118 Bde moving to Training Area. Arrangements made to supply as usual at Refilling Point	ppl
	5.6.17 to		Routine work	ppl
	9.6.17	11-0pm	Division now in Light Camps. The army having taken over a portion of the Second Army front. The neighbourhood is being shelled. Some shells have fallen in the vicinity of the camps but not damage has been	ppl
	10.6.17	11-0pm	done to prepare to move. Division now under XVIII Corps	ppl
	to 16.6.17	11-0pm	Routine work. A. Dumps and Workshops inspected by General Cuninghame.	ppl
	23.6.17	11-0pm		ppl
	24.6.17	11-0pm	Visited 118 Brigade in Training Area. Inspected all vehicles of the Brigade as they are shortly returning to the line and it was reported the they were in a bad state. I was afterwards by ex C/Staff Offr from the 4 Army found a great many total required immediate attention. This information was very kept to Sucnham the conflict ordering consum for the brigade	ppl

1875 Wt. W593/826 1,000,000 4/15. J.B.C.&A. A.D.S.S./Forms/C.2118.

WAR DIARY
or
INTELLIGENCE SUMMARY
(Erase heading not required.)

Army Form C. 2118

Place	Date	Hour	Summary of Events and Information	Remarks and references to Appendices
3rd 38 A.D.S.	25.6.17	11 am	Had a meeting of O. Hookers of 117 Bde who are nearly hot to carry on without. Reviewed all returning medical stocking in especially equipment in the carrantines esp like above on attached Inspection details of 117 Bde — found some what unsatisfactory. Brigade an leave, nine to having men.	[X]
	21.6.17 11 pm			[X]
	30.6.17 8 pm		Routine work. Bulled move from PROVEN to PESELHOEK.	[X]
			There has been a very bad muddle in regards to supply of Ordnance Stores. The Brigade in the Training Area has been supplied without a hitch but the lorries have not returned till late in the evening and therefore making return work for the Brigade W.O. I have therefore considered it inadvisable to accumulate the said items to temporarily transfer them to I. Bde in close touch and it is facilitated by the units themselves.	[X]

B.P.M.R. 6H
RADMS. 39 Div

WAR DIARY
INTELLIGENCE SUMMARY

of CAPT. D.R. SMITH
D.A.D.O.S.
39. DIVISION

Vol 17

Army Form C. 2118
Instructions regarding War Diaries and Intelligence Summaries are contained in F.S. Regs., Part II. and the Staff Manual respectively. Title Pages will be prepared in manuscript.

(Erase heading not required.)

Place	Date	Hour	Summary of Events and Information	Remarks and references to Appendices
Sha. 98				
Hzd.6.3	1.7.17	11-9pm	17 Bde. moving to training area. Shoes will be sent by lorry to Reffiling Point	
"	2.7.17	11-9pm	Visited Brval Troops.	
"	3.7.17	"	11 received Bn Bn attached from XVIII Corps Troops for administration	
"	4.7.17	"	1/2 K.O.Y.L.I. attached from 31st Divn.	
"	"	"	9 York & Lancs " " 17th "	
"	"	"	1st Northumberland Fus. Bn " " "	
"	6.7.17	"	51 Divisional Artillery attached for administration. Dump Shelled	
"	6.7.17	11:30	Visited Refilling Point. Dump Shelled	
"	"	"	1st Divisional Artillery Reg. — No Casualties	
"	7.7.17	11-9pm	Visited Railhead. Brought around of stores arrived including Rob Roddy	
"	"	"	3 Sketches etc.	
"	6.7.17	11-9pm	Rankin took Dump Shelled	
"	11.7.17	"	Conference with Quartermasters of 118 Bde. Outs atrophy.	
"	12.7.17	"	Shell test in Camp — Casualties 9 Cow t' hor."	
"	16.7.17	"	51 Div Artillery moved to 51 Divinion	
"	16.7.17	"	Tracks unité in Training Area	
"	19.7.17	11-9pm	Attended Expences at Halgarkes 29 Div.	

1875 Wt. W593/826 1,000,000 4/15 J.B.C. & A. A.D.S.S./Forms/C. 2118.

WAR DIARY / INTELLIGENCE SUMMARY

Army Form C. 2118

Place	Date	Hour	Summary of Events and Information	Remarks and references to Appendices
Abeele A.7.A.5.3	21.7.17	11-8pm	998 Recruits from England. Attended Conference at Corps.	
"	22.7.17	11-8pm	In view of heavy Casualties have despatched a Cony to CALAIS to collect & stores urgently required.	
"	23.7.17	11-8pm	Lony returned with the majority of the stores. All ammunition stores for these Batteries supplied. Very heavy day for general stores. Over 50 tons handled and distributed.	
"	24.7.17	11-8pm	48 DAC Artillery transferred to 48 Division.	
"	25.7.17	11-8pm	Attended Conference at Divisional Headquarters.	
"	26.7.17	11-8pm	Visited Railway Sidings, Pack & Tanks of Second Army troops.	
"	27.7.17	11-8pm	Visited Barbogne & forward material.	
"	28.7.17	11-8pm	Attended Conference at Corps.	
"	29.7.17	11-8pm	Visited Railhead & Tank.	
"	30.7.17	11-8pm	Reviewed all obtaining demands. Borrow & supplies. Nothing obtaining what will affect the fighting efficiency of the unit.	
"	31.7.17	11-8pm	2 Coy. 5" Divn Train required by H. of Comds to replace others damaged by Shell fire.	

Army Form C. 2118

WAR DIARY
INTELLIGENCE SUMMARY
(Erase heading not required.)

Place	Date	Hour	Summary of Events and Information	Remarks and references to Appendices
	31.7.17		This has been an extremely busy month. The preparation for the attack has necessitated large bounds in here - many additional items such as Rct/Paddy, Burn Cornards 18 pr + 4.5 Hrs, Rifles Mine, Bomb Grenades, Hot Food Containers etc have been drawn and issued. The attachment of no 50 additional units has made a great deal of extra work but the supply has been maintained without interruption. In addition 900 Carriers for Machine Gun Belt Box are manufactured in the Shops.	

A.Atherton Capt
D.A.O.O. 39 Div

WAR DIARY or INTELLIGENCE SUMMARY

Army Form C. 2118

OF CAPT. D.R. SMITH
D.A.D.O.S.
29 DIV.

Place	Date	Hour	Summary of Events and Information	Remarks and references to Appendices
Sheet 29 A.22.d.5.3	1.9.17	1.8.17 to 8pm	Third Battle of Ypres still continues. Divisions heavily engaged. 5 Lewis and Stokes guns reported to replace. These were replaced within 6 hours.	10/18
"	2.9.17	"	9 Lewis & 17 Vickers Gun regiments detachables kept to Q.M. R.E. delivered to units within 6 hrs. Lewis Q.M. Stores.	
"	3.9.17	"	Visited Rouleur. 27 Lewis Guns repaired & replaced anything were processes of yesterday. These guns were issued to units tonight by 6 army.	
"	4.9.17	"	Attended a Conference at Corps. Unit will shortly be coming out. Bde. inform me clothing is in a deplorable condition. Am arranging to issue Helmets for clothing. 29 Lewis Vickers [Guns]? Have been replaced.	
"	5.9.17	"	Lorries returned from Calais at 6.30am. Details have to make hill to made by 2.0 am. Knowns worked this over the matter is arranged of the Lewis [Guns]	10/18

WAR DIARY
INTELLIGENCE SUMMARY

Army Form C. 2118

Place	Date	Hour	Summary of Events and Information	Remarks and references to Appendices
Sheet 28 H22.d.5.3.	6.8.17	11-3pm	Clothing worn this morning. Boots hold older all baggage rendered useless. To enforce preparing to move to Second Army. Artillery will remain to be attached to 148 Bde.	AE1
METEREN	7.8.17	11-3pm	Division move to METEREN and came under orders of I Corps. All stores M.T.'s moving too move allotted.	AE1
"	8.8.17	11-3pm	Strength will require a good deal of stores. Have worked all units with a view of producing indents.	
"	9.8.17	11-3pm	Convoy despatched to Calais for Stores. A good quantity of stores are required viz 250 Rifles, 1000 Mills Gaiters, 250 Entrench. 930 Binoculars, 570 Periscopes, 220 Very Pistols too Gas Masks. Various Indus are obtained practically all stores required.	AE1
"	10.8.17	11-3pm	Convoy returned and distribution has commenced.	AE1
"	11.8.17	11-3pm	Lorry again sent to Base for Re. Equipment. A good number of Warm Respirators are required to replace all anomalies one and with Men's wire. Rifle are in a very bad state owing to weather conditions. All Lewis & Lichen guns had again a thorough overhaul.	AE1

Army Form C. 2118

WAR DIARY
or
INTELLIGENCE SUMMARY
(Erase heading not required.)

Instructions regarding War Diaries and Intelligence Summaries are contained in F. S. Regs., Part II. and the Staff Manual respectively. Title Pages will be prepared in manuscript.

Place	Date	Hour	Summary of Events and Information	Remarks and references to Appendices
METEREN	16.5.17	2pm	Visited Railhead Canin. 116 Bde moved to forward area	
"	18.5.17	"	Visited A.D.S. XVIII Corps. 117 Bde moved to relieve Bde of 41st Div.	
"	14.5.17	"	118 Bde moves to forward area. Visited Ordnance 41st Division.	
WESTOUTRE	15.5.17		Office and dumps move to WESTOUTRE being over from 41st Division. Following units attached for administration. 1st Brigade (T) by R.E. 175 (T) by R.E. 41st Bearer Fd. Ban. Hd. III. 45.5.6 Eden Sqn.	
"	16.5.17	9pm	Visited ESTAIRE and DUNKERQUE Railway Ordnance Stores.	
"	19.5.17	"	Visited units of Division	
"	20.5.17	9pm	41st Div R.A. was attached for administration	
"	21.5.17	11-2pm	Visited Railhead units	
"	23.5.17	11-8pm	R.A. (39) was attached. Visited Staff Sgt. and Batteries. They have lost a great deal of equipment	
"	23.5.17	11-9pm	Visited R.A. units	
"	24.5.17	11-9pm	190 Bde was D.Arty moved to 41st Division	
"	25.5.17	11-9pm	Conference with Quartermaster Sgts of Artillery as to ways of obtaining indents immediately	

Army Form C. 2118

WAR DIARY
or
INTELLIGENCE SUMMARY
(Erase heading not required.)

Instructions regarding War Diaries and Intelligence Summaries are contained in F.S. Regs., Part II. and the Staff Manual respectively. Title Pages will be prepared in manuscript.

Place	Date	Hour	Summary of Events and Information	Remarks and references to Appendices
WESTOUTRE	26.8.17	11 p.m.	Orders received from R.A. write out an ordering lorries & others for hosing	
"	27.8.17	11 p.m.	Convoy went to CALAIS tonight	
"	28.8.17	11 p.m.	Visited billets and interviewed all Comp. Officers. Lorries will retain drivers with a great amount of technical equipment. Convoy returned. R.A. will be purchasing re-equipped	
"	29.8.17	11 p.m.	1st 45 below hrs moved to 7 Tk Bps Tps	
"	30.8.17	11 p.m.	229 - 253 - 257 Tk Coys & 19 M.d.d.sx from 11 Div for demonstration	
"	31.8.17	11 p.m.	This has been exceptionally heavy work. The division has been heavily engaged and very severe casualties. Consequently when the units were withdrawn from the line they had to be practically reclothed and the majority of their equipment was either destroyed by shell fire or lost. In keeping the demand for clothing dispatched home to Calais and stuff arrived in time to forward units as they came out of the line. The Bdes being supplied with shell fire. The Infantry including Machine Gun Companies	

1875 Wt. W593/826 1,000,000 4/15 J.B.C. & A. A.D.S.S./Forms/C. 2118.

WAR DIARY
INTELLIGENCE SUMMARY
(Erase heading not required.)

Army Form C. 2118

Place	Date	Hour	Summary of Events and Information	Remarks and references to Appendices
			and Trench Mortar Batteries have re-equipped and are able to go into action with all Arms affecting the fighting efficiency. The requirements of these units have altered so greatly owing to the fact that forever to be attacked a lot in our act to all units during the stunt soleil never fortify again replacing. The total are filled in and where immediately the demands being considered and attention to have. This system undoubtedly saving many days delay.	

O.P. Smith Capt
D.A.D.V.S. 39 Dn

WAR DIARY
INTELLIGENCE SUMMARY
OF CAPT D.R SMITH
DADOS 39 Div

Army Form C. 2118

Place	Date	Hour	Summary of Events and Information	Remarks and references to Appendices
WESTOUTRE	1.7.17	10.0am	Conference with 116 Brigade Quartermasters - QOC 117 Brigade called re M.G. Store - Proposed sending to Calais	
"	2.10.17	"	Conference at 117 Bde Hdq. with Quartermasters. Lorry left for Calais	
"	3.10.17	"	Lorry returned from Calais with available stores for 117 Bde. Following units transferred to I Corps Troops :- 4 Canada Res Bath. 11 Elswy Coy. 1/1 Nld Res Coy. 1/2 & 46 Res Coy. 1/2 & 45 Lab Coy.	
"	4.10.17	"	Visited units	
"	5.10.17	"	Following units attached from 2nd Don :- 14 Northumberlane Fus. 97.98. 126 Field Coy. R.E. Worked late re Battle Order	
"	6.10.17	"	Visited that line. Transferred out O.C. 39 D/C Train	
"	7.10.17	"	Following units transferred from us o1 D.A.C. :- Hdqs Battery. 190 Bde R.F.A. also 13 & 4th Res Z. Bathn.	
"	8.10.17	"	17 Amm. Sub Park transferred the administration from I Corps Troops	
"	9.10.17	"	Visited units re Buffaloes	
"	10.10.17	"	Proposed Buff Orders Buses re nowing transport. New arrangement for two dumps. 51.03 Bde Artillery was attached for administration also 20% M.G. Coy from I Corps Troops	

WAR DIARY
INTELLIGENCE SUMMARY
(Erase heading not required.)

Army Form C. 2118

Place	Date	Hour	Summary of Events and Information	Remarks and references to Appendices
WESTOUTRE	11/10/17	10.0 pm	Collected Cliff Cadrew - Chilibeth 21.01 Bn in huts and followed 7th & 3rd Brigade on regains. Then have been shortened.	App/
DE ZON CAMP Sheet 25 H.15.a.4.9.	12.10.17	9.0 pm	Moved to De Zon Camp. 21 Coy had of Ohm	App/
	13.10.17	8.0 pm	Parties to Butte Ohm - three in & Chap'y & m.of Br.	App/
	14.10.17	nil	Visited there Ambulances & other regions for improving hosp.	App/
	15.10.17	11.0 pm	Dress & Carriage arrangements for 21/d & R.A. War and Salvage in Regiment & the attacks by of tanks.	App/
	16.10.17	11.0 pm	All units are now practically equipped for stretcher bearer Brigade & are all ready for further advance when to be renewed.	App/
	17.10.17	10.0 pm	R.A. regains 3 Bde Light Carriers. Have more bits Brace. Nil available	App/
	18.10.17	11.0 pm	between Collected form that Army Own Park	App/
	19.10.17	11.0 pm	See Ordnance Railhead Open at Oxderdom. A. Vischer Railhead. Track lake - Vischer Forward Cars Park and arrange searching of Salvage	App/
	20.10.17	11.0 pm	Visited forward area	App/
	21.10.17	11.0 pm	117 Brigade in attacks	App/
	22.10.17	11.0 pm	Visited 117 Bde Transport lines. Egan B.M.C to arrange new arrangement details	App/
	23.10.17	11 a.pm	Visited A.D.s of 117 Bde - will have most army & track	App/

WAR DIARY
or
INTELLIGENCE SUMMARY
(Erase heading not required.)

Army Form C. 2118

Instructions regarding War Diaries and Intelligence Summaries are contained in F.S. Regs, Part II. and the Staff Manual respectively. Title Pages will be prepared in manuscript.

Place	Date	Hour	Summary of Events and Information	Remarks and references to Appendices
DE ZON CNR P	25.10.17	11-3pm	All ranks received out-residence. Lorries sent to Calais to collect all available stores. Party ref. arranging programme of stores at other regiments.	
RENINGHELST	26.10.17	11-3pm	Bef 116 + 118 Bdes for infantry staff. Moved with difficulty to hrs camp. 26 Conf. Conf. much trouble. C.O.O. Calais.	
	26.10.17	11-3pm	Conveyance from Calais with stores for 117 Bde. The Bgenes re-equipped by 10-3pm and ready for line. Few batteries of the Bde moved into line. 116 + 118 Bde in Division still refitting.	
	27.10.17	11-3pm	Morning Headquart moves to ST. JANS CAPELL hrs IX Corps from 10.0 am. Marched C.O.O. IX Corps + D.A.D.O.S. 37 Divn. Moved office to make up to hrs camp. Bdes re ordnance.	
ST. JANS CAPELL	28.10.17	11-3pm	Visited Bdes. Looking intact.	
	29.10.17	11-3pm	Visited Bdes. Dependable. Lorries to Calais for Ord. Stores. C.O.O. IX Corps.	
	30.10.17	11-3pm		
	31.10.17	11-3pm	The line again has an extremely heavy march. The divisions in the line all the time and fought this hard. The 117 Bde are re-equipped and this 2 days. I regret to report that the kits are actually put into line and all times regiments complete.	

R. M. Smith Capt
D.A.D.O.S. 29 Division

WAR DIARY
INTELLIGENCE SUMMARY
(Erase heading not required.)

Army Form C. 2118

of CAPT. D.R. SMITH
O.A.D.O.S. 39 DIV

Vol 20

Place	Date	Hour	Summary of Events and Information	Remarks and references to Appendices
ST. JAN'S CAPEL	1.10.17 to 8pm		Visited Rubber units	
	2.10.17	"	Reported Transport of 117 Bde. Extn. J 17 NWk + Chief Ranger of Kmt. Out to H.Q.M.	
	3.10.17	"	Amm returns from Calais. Distribution of stoves & ovens, pressing + 3s bins. I tub m 1.6.?	
			N/R unit at Rubber.	
			Divisions re-equipped.	
	3.10.17	"	2 hr Market orders? from Armee Corps troops. Enrolment of Market.	
	4.10.17	"	Visited 117 Bde. - Saw Market orders	
	5.10.17	"	Market delivered to units	
	6.10.17	"	Visited Rubber	
	7.10.17	"	Market as per Transport & Linen	
	8.10.17	"	Conference with Q.M. of 117 Bde. + 116 Bde.	
	9.10.17	"	Visited units	
	10.10.17	"	Market Rubber units	
	11.10.17	"	To visit 118 Bde. - WOODKOYUM	
	12.10.17	"	On Leave to England	
	13.10.17 to	"	Being the largest amount of roads	
	15.10.17	"	clothing emitted and recovered. Large conference to DE ZON CAMP	
			Start of M.B.M.W.G on 15th October.	
			Nothing of importance to report except the HQ HLN clothing ordnance rep?	
			could be visited daily. The amount of non accounting of HQ may be large	
			amount of sunk clothing Recovered.	
			B.R. Smith Capt	
DE ZON CAMP	26.10.17 to			
Sheet 28	31.10.17			D.A.D.O.S. 39 Div
M.28.a.g.				

WAR DIARY
INTELLIGENCE SUMMARY
(Erase heading not required.)

Army Form C. 2118

of CAPT D.R. SMITH D.A.D.O.S 29 DIV

Vol 21

Place	Date	Hour	Summary of Events and Information	Remarks and references to Appendices
DE ZON CAMP M.18.A.4.9	1.11.17	10 pm	Visited units of 117 Bde. Salvage Dump	TRI
"	2.11.17	"	Visited Run. Boot Drying Room. Drier arranged to work up men to work it. Drying Room has been erected by R. Engineers. The Boots are dried by a new method. They are placed on metal plates which let air in forced thro'. By this method the boots are not greatly injured	TRI
"	3.11.17	"	Visited Brigade Schools & Divisional Wing & Corps Reinforcement Camps	TRI
"	4.11.17	"	Letter of Importance	TRI
"	10.11.17	"	Visited 117 Bde. Salvage Dump	TRI
"	11.11.17	"	Visited 3 Sutn. in 7th Bde Artillery. The Artillery is holding up and is probably going to ITALY. Have wired have the Arty. Helmets, Clothing respirators, phosphor all serial alike. Three phases to D.A.D.O.S. 19th D.V. in May am forwarding to Lt. area. Lt. TLEGGATT A.O.D. proved his instruction manual officer of 7 D.V. Derbyshire to BLARINGHEM to join 19th D.V.	TRI
"	12.11.17	"	Visited Railhead. Stores & vehicles arrived for 7 D.V. R.A. Rearranged to 19th Div. Dump in came under the administration of IX Corps.	TRI
"	14.11.17	"	Visited 117 Bde and Run. Boot Drying Room. Moved V.H.T. Rich. Bullock 17th Div. Mtg.	TRI
"	15.11.17	"	Bivouac. Moving to WESTOUTRE. Visited the village and inspected dumps. Arranged with fillers. Officers moved to WESTOUTRE. Have taken on O.O. Capt. Turpin 7b O.O. King	TRI
WESTOUTRE M.11.7			Dumps shifts. offer	TRI

Army in Rear

Army Form C. 2118

WAR DIARY
or
INTELLIGENCE SUMMARY
(Erase heading not required.)

Instructions regarding War Diaries and Intelligence Summaries are contained in F. S. Regs., Part II. and the Staff Manual respectively. Title Pages will be prepared in manuscript.

Place	Date	Hour	Summary of Events and Information	Remarks and references to Appendices
WESTOUTRE	17.11.17	11-30am	Visited A.D.V.S. IX Corps units of 118 Bde. Visited 7th Bde Troops.	
"	18.11.17	"	Visited units rendered. Visited Bde. Troops.	
"	19.11.17	"	D. LEGGATT left for ESTAPLES. He has returned to general duty. He also saw the transport officer, Salvage etc. Visited A.D.V.S IX Corps. Lt.Col. GOOD VIII Corps. Major/.../ The artillery of the Division are moving to VIII Corps area. About 160 men of the R.F.A. too have moved to be exchanged at once. The A.D.V.S. says the clothing is unfortunately not dangerous to the wearer. I am sending every horse that tends to [...] to clothing and [...] the matter to A.D.V.S. IX Corps. The horses use a big question, ie. the artillery maintenance to troops engage against the latest effects of the clothing is really difficult. Reserves will abide & be held in [...] immediate exchange. Visited D.A.D.O.S. 33 Div with reference to transferring of Artillery to Corps. Transferred artillery to 33 Div on arrival by the Corps.	
"	20.11.17	"	A.V.C. (Chapman) & M. Rivey. Visited Ruckham & Bde.	
"	21.11.17	"	Visited STEENVOORDE. The division will probably move to this area.	
"	22.11.17	"	Pony Cl. Racing meeting for Tailors Staff.	
"	23.11.17	"	Visited STEENVOORDE. Interviewed Brigadier (Name?) D.A.D.O.S. 30 Division. Hoer HQ R.E. 225, 227 & 264 Field Coys, the 32 Division.	
"	24.11.17	"	Visited units [...] Div.	
"	25.11.17	"	Visited [...] units.	

Army Form C. 2118

WAR DIARY
or
INTELLIGENCE SUMMARY
(Erase heading not required.)

Place	Date	Hour	Summary of Events and Information	Remarks and references to Appendices
WESTOUTRE	26.11.17	11.30 pm	Many stores to STEENVOORDE during the evening of the DADOS 30 Div. to be placed in Steenvoorde. Visited 117 Bde Hd. qurs.	
STEENVOORDE	27.11.17		Route demands of store, office at 2 new dumps. Supply stores received from unit. established rating 117 bde. officers and troops stores. Horses also unit established 116 Bde + units.	
"	28.11.17		Boney caps arranged dumps, workshops. Visited 116 Bde + units.	
"	29.11.17		Visited E.O.H.	
"	30.11.17		Visited 6 O.D. Fy byres. A later Sept Dr. has started his march & slowly I have lost over 100 to mis. of 229 Bo of prelloes from overcoats returned by units. 92 great coats, 10 jackets and 76 trausers have been repaired ready to reissued.	

Approved By Col Brown 39 Div.

WAR DIARY OF CAPT D.R. SMITH Army Form C. 2118
INTELLIGENCE SUMMARY   D.A.D.O.S. 29 D.V.
(Erase heading not required.)

Instructions regarding War Diaries and Intelligence Summaries are contained in F.S. Regs., Part II. and the Staff Manual respectively. Title Pages will be prepared in manuscript.

Place	Date	Hour	Summary of Events and Information	Remarks and references to Appendices
STEENVOORDE	1.12.17 to 8.12.17	10·0 pm	Nothing of importance to report – Visited units and Can. Cavalry Brigade in VIII Corps area re the catching of salvage.	
NEILLES LEZ BLEQUIN	9.12.17	11·0 am	Division moving to rest area & under Orders of L. of C. Area – travel today.	
	10.12.17	10·0 pm	Visited Div. Salvage & refilling point.	
	11.12.17	" "	Visited units with a view to obtaining wants re clothing	
	12.12.17	7·0 pm	Visited C.O.O. CALAIS. Requested him to see to our available stores in order that units may be completed so far as possible before returning to the line.	
	13.12.17 to 21.12.17		Routine Work. Have visited units. A great deal of stores have been received and units are practically re-equipped.	

D.R. Smith Capt
D.A.D.O.S. 29 Div.

Army Form C. 2118

WAR DIARY
or
INTELLIGENCE SUMMARY

OF CAPT D.R SMITH
D.A.D.O.S. Bg Dil.

(Erase heading not required.)

Instructions regarding War Diaries and Intelligence Summaries are contained in F. S. Regs., Part II. and the Staff Manual respectively. Title Pages will be prepared in manuscript.

Place	Date	Hour	Summary of Events and Information	Remarks and references to Appendices
A.D.d.5	3.1.18 to 6.1.18		Was attending an Ammunition Course at No.1st Ordnance Depot. During this time Cpl Burrows moved from NIELLES LEZ BLEQUIN to F. Echn Stores and relieved the 32 Div Burrows in the line. The move was kept for three days to settle conditions. Office kept [?] when entering Stores lorries. 9 days of move.	
Obd 28.				
"	14.1.18	10.4pm	had on 1st int. g.s. lorries attached stores from Railhead. 3 loads at P'head 32 Div Ardtllery move for ammunition as & want. These formations ltd on. Others was relieved of A.D.C lorries nuntrance[?] Ammy from Depots.	✓
	15.1.18	10.3pm	These formations off-loaded motors.	✓
	16.1.18	10pm	These formations off again. Large amount of Stores coming from the [?] [?] Railhead and rail.	✓
	17.1.18	10.3pm	Vickers Railhead and rail.	✓
	18.1.18	10.3pm	Visited CALAIS on R Burrows will in all probability move back to 4 high Army area. Arranged to send lorries to effect return and made arrangement for transfer of stores ext to 32 Division.	✓
	19.1.18	10.3pm	32 Div Ardllry move to 32 Division.	✓

WAR DIARY

INTELLIGENCE SUMMARY

(Erase heading not required.)

Army Form C. 2118

CAPT- D.R. SMITH
D.A.D.O.S. 39 DIV.

Vol 23

Place	Date	Hour	Summary of Events and Information	Remarks and references to Appendices
A.D.D.O.S. Oct 28	20/1/18	11 a.m.	Vickers Railhead. Taken precautions abt: a. all storerooms. Nothing apparently right by "B" Echk army to extreme north. Confirm arranged to send Clerk to have the clothing and exchange as arrival lorries despatched. Proceeded today to AMIENS to make necessary arrangements to bring on.	SM
AMIENS	22.1.18	"	Visited D.D.O.S. Fifth Army. D.A.D.O.S. of Divisions. Railhead and portable refilling points. Learn returned to Dumps of A.D.O.S. 3. all clothing and urgent stores issued. Few lorries left for rear area.	SM
AMIENS	23.1.18	"	Taken over Office & dumps of 14th Division. Base service to "Commence Supply" normal routine. Divisional A.D.O.S. VII Corps & Division is moving to VII Corps area and releasing 9th Div. Made necessary arrangements for taking over dumps etc are an moving to NURLU on a.m. of	SM
MERICOURT Sr. SOMME	24.1.18 to 30.1.18	"		SM

F.M. Smith Capt
DADOS 39 Div

Army Form C. 2118

of CAPT D.I.R. SMITH
D.A.D.O.S. 29 D.V.

WAR DIARY
or
INTELLIGENCE SUMMARY
(Erase heading not required.)

14

Place	Date	Hour	Summary of Events and Information	Remarks and references to Appendices
NURLU	1.2.18		At Nurlu. During whole time Nurlu is shelved the 9 F.A. Dumain, F.A. Coys had taken over everything move to NURLU a lot a great deal of time away from them. Busy to improve my time for everything. So the client and various in one day.	
	16.2.18		12 Divn. all of M/T to and D.of Schraden. Came later to see despatched to Ruithen.	
	17.2.18	4.45pm	Visited motor. clothes works. Interior both of Byard Corps Ruithen bath.	
	18.2.18	"	Visited ADOS F.A. Corps. use ADOS. Light hvy. in back outward.	
	19.2.18	"	Ruithen as unstart. Ruithen buts.	
	20.2.18	10.8p	N. Then Incomme as it is now busy.	
	21.2.18	10.8p	"	
	22.2.18	10.8p	Visited Ruithen. PERSONS and N.S. Bn. Regt.	
	23.2.18	10.8p	Then Executive offer in. Real difficulty in obtaining transport to move stores from Ruithen. Issued Ordnance sup.	
	24.2.18	10.8p	Ruithen book	

Army Form C. 2118

WAR DIARY
or
INTELLIGENCE SUMMARY
(Erase heading not required.)

Instructions regarding War Diaries and Intelligence Summaries are contained in F. S. Regs., Part II. and the Staff Manual respectively. Title Pages will be prepared in manuscript.

Place	Date	Hour	Summary of Events and Information	Remarks and references to Appendices
NURLU	25.2.19	11-0pm	[illegible] arrives to [illegible] etc.	
	26.2.19	0.30pm	Officers Conference at Bg Orders.	
	27.2.19	11.0am	Parties sent. Entrance of Prisoners at 7 Officers	
	28.2.19	11.0am	[illegible]	

J.V.Smith Lt.
Orders 29. Bn.

WAR DIARY
INTELLIGENCE SUMMARY
(Erase heading not required.)

Army Form C. 2118

1 CAPT D.R. SMITH
D.A.D.O.S. 29 D[ivision]

Vol 25

Place	Date	Hour	Summary of Events and Information	Remarks and references to Appendices
NURLU	1.3.18 to 2.3.18	10-1pm	Normal	
"	3.3.18	"	Attended Conference of Forage MKT & II & Fld 107 types	
"	4.3.18	"	Commenced to convert 5000 [gardens] in Commr's Charge. There are to be used in this area for the destruction of enemy tanks.	
"	5.3.18	"	"	
"	7.3.18	"	Visited O/c A.O.C. Depots ROUEN & C.O.O. ROUEN	
"	8.3.18	"	Normal	
"	9.3.18.10.3.18	"	"	
"	11.3.18	"	Division being relieved by 9th Division. Handed over dumps etc to A.D. Canadn 1 Cavalry Dvn. Also him to HQ AOT ALLAINES with B.H.Q.	
"	12.3.18 10.17am	10.17am Attack rifle & fairly moved		
HAUT ALLAINES	13.3.18 10-1pm	Movements etc		
"	14.3.18 to 19.3.18	"	Normal	
"	20.3.18	"	"	
"	21.3.18	"	Very heavy bombardment. Enemy attacking. Division is in G.H.Q reserve. All expected to go into line for men. To turn of stores recd from here. Partly moved to [unit]	

WAR DIARY
INTELLIGENCE SUMMARY

Army Form C. 2118

of CAPT D.R. SMITH
D.A.D.O.S. 39 DIVISION D/15/07

Place	Date	Hour	Summary of Events and Information	Remarks and references to Appendices
HAUT ALLAINES	22.3.18	12.0 midnight	Great too much of S.D. at 11.0 am. No. 1 Fd Hosp Ambulance of former crew also Bn. No. 4 115 Fld at LONGAVESNES. A hty of heavy artillery in position in field engaging things as in action any firing. Bugs transport in the rounds at a time. Received orders from CRE of D.G.E. to move to CLERY sur SOMME - Commenced move at 11.0 pm and hope to remove all others -	
MARICOURT	23.3.18	12.0 midnight	All other closed including Office - 16 hrs/tables - SHQ moved to CLERY sur SOMME & at 11.0 am marched one to move to MARICOURT. Commenced to move at 11.0 am. and all stores cleared by 10.0 pm. The move was greatly hampered by the great amount of traffic on road. M.O. this firm every aeroplane also causing inconvenience. Personal left behind to guard remaining stores had to destroy them owing to shells fire are M.O. this from aeroplanes. Stores sent to clear the store was taken back by TRAFFIC Officer as it was too dangerous to proceed further in the direction of CLERY.	
CHUIGNES - BRAY-PROYART ROAD	24.3.18	12.0 midnight	Left MARICOURT at 3.0 am for BRAY-PROYART Road. Dump being finally broken. Proceeded with all important stores & left personnel (2 men) also protected by a platoon other in charge of removing other Ordnance Stores any thing 2 stores they had of essentially before leave owing to enemy to close	

Army Form C. 2118

WAR DIARY
/ CAPT. D.R SMITH
INTELLIGENCE SUMMARY
D.A.D.O.S 39 DIV.

(Erase heading not required.)

Place	Date	Hour	Summary of Events and Information	Remarks and references to Appendices
CHUIGNES BRAY-PRONART ROAD	25.3.18	9.0 pm	Arrived at Proyart of HQ camp at Bray Proyart Road at 4.0 am. and then to get into touch with D.M.S. etc. were unbroken by Two Major of Bray to be at CORBIE. Moved to CORBIE at 6.0 am. & found BAQ here at FRISE. Rumours reported that washing gone with regtl equipment & defended trains to Gen Staff to collect. Subsequently moving to a gun dump near BRAY. after some search found the M.G. Park and received 16 Vickers complete also laboriously oil. 31 Lewis guns here also been drawn and are being issued. B.H.Q. moved to CHUIGNOLLES have moved to Pty O. Camp early the morning. 31 Lewis guns have moved many kept out early morning. The following which were repaired and advanced

225 In Ch Coy. G.S. Wagon. 1. Parker Wagon. 2. Wagons Limbered R.E. 4.
606o Bn. 1. Parker Bn. 1. Bucket. 4.
13 Glosters 1 Kitchen Trawling. 207 Field Coy. Parker Wagon 1.
Lagros Limbers R.E. 2. No.1. Parties D.A.C. 1 G.S Wagon.

Am on way to CERISY. & motorbars sent from De Kaing etc.
Have been unable to even been to MARICOURT owing to the fact they have been engaged all day and tons. | |

WAR DIARY
INTELLIGENCE SUMMARY

Army Form C. 2118

OF CAPT D.R.SMITH
D.A.D.O.S. 39 Div

Place	Date	Hour	Summary of Events and Information	Remarks and references to Appendices
HAMELETTE	26.5.18	9.0 p.m.	Arrived at CERISY at 1.0 am. Ohs. of train - bomb hopper - some to move to HAMELETTE at 9.0 a.m. to the nearton wagon 116 Bde with rt. wh. t 8 Leric guns. also 117 Bde w.t at which remained a here. also formouris made to temp equipment, shoe mrnings, blankets, steel shr. taken? Rabban.	set
BOVES	27.5.18	8.0 pm	Arrived at BOVES at 5.0 am. Recd an urgent wire at 2.0 a.m. (HAMELETTE) from D.C. HQ to move without delay to BOVES a enemy had overrun SAILLY LEE-SEC. Ohm broken and things chance by 2.30 a.m. On arrived at the town at 5.0 a.m. could not get a bomb at once. found suitable place at 11.0 am. Was also collected 12 Vickers complete 8 Lewis complete and 500 Magazine am issued to out enemy. Magazine ham been issued to P.O.O. and D.A.C. Armr? ken ken sent to and 7 Magazine will be ready to cart o armt. This will greatly aid our same hore in the line. flying shells Armre HG Batn, 6 bayns L.P.S. 2 Travelling Kitchens 1 bath cart 1 Bomb Cart for A/174 Bde. Vichen Rakeup. Vickers Ruckhan. fld wheel stampers 15/5/18 the armour magazine, stol. int col. off loan- ent int colas of Magazine, stol. not collected from Gun opals of issued.	off
"	28/5/18	1.5 pm		

WAR DIARY / CAPT D.R. SMITH

INTELLIGENCE SUMMARY D.A.D.O.S. 39 Div.

Army Form C. 2118

(Erase heading not required.)

Instructions regarding War Diaries and Intelligence Summaries are contained in F.S. Regs., Part II. and the Staff Manual respectively. Title Pages will be prepared in manuscript.

Place	Date	Hour	Summary of Events and Information	Remarks and references to Appendices
BOVES	29/3/18		Visited Quartermasters and Brigade to ascertain urgent requirements. Divisional transport still in the line. Out at present offering aid – Chief item requires Boots, socks, oil flannelette. Previous had always been made known.	XX
"	30/3/18		Visited DDOS 4th Army. ADOS 5th Corps. All which obtain from welfare.	XX
St FUSCIEN	1/4/18		From line today – 16 tons of stores saved, this was collected but only a portable and half tent used items to reorganise available. Own army out of line and outfit will be held ready. One out a long Lt ABBEVILLE to draw for our will issue to suit all circulating and knows nothing.	XX

S.R. Smith Capt
D.A.D.O.S. 39 Div.

WAR DIARY or INTELLIGENCE SUMMARY

of CAPT. D. R. SMITH Army Form C. 2118
D.A.D.O.S. 39 DIV

Vol 26

Place	Date	Hour	Summary of Events and Information	Remarks and references to Appendices
GUIGNEMICOURT	1/4/18	11-4pm	Moved from St Sauveur the morning. Division has most of the line now concentrating at LONGUEAU then AMIENS. During the night I got for 5000 prs of socks. These arrived 9.0 am. Showed to all unit by 10.0 am. also shirts. Every man gets a complete outfit. Gds Bn. Staff orders - Deputies spare want to hrs for clothing. however, S.C. has been there, has [?] the forms that those items but pointed out being for R.U.E. tomorrow.	[?]
"	2/5/18	1.0 midnight	Left for R.U.E. - there cancelled during morning - have all day at R.U.E. Lengthy Comyns with C.O.O HEDERVILLE to supply Scotland. Grand value	[?]
OISEMONT	3/4/5/18	10 midnight	Moved to the Area today. Division has given me Hearse Crews. The lorries despatched to LE TREPORT for Blankets which have as undertaking what has been ordered from [?] at Abbeville.	[?]
	4/5/18		Have arranged to [?] above Hearse trunks by Lorry & Railed Regulation of off metals to complete refitting stores to be in this wake of [?] Stores closed on Monday. ALLY Sr SOMME	[?]

Army Form C. 2118

WAR DIARY
of CAPT D.R SMITH
INTELLIGENCE SUMMARY D.A.D.O.S. 39 Div.
(Erase heading not required.)

Instructions regarding War Diaries and Intelligence Summaries are contained in F.S. Regs., Part II. and the Staff Manual respectively. Title Pages will be prepared in manuscript.

Place	Date	Hour	Summary of Events and Information	Remarks and references to Appendices
DISEMONT	6.4.15		Kept all wards resorted. Staff working all night. Everything going all to my own morning. Waken outs - Blake Pte m.d. without any error.	
CALAIS	6.4.15	1.0 pm	Arrived Left with O.P. Blair. Chief back from OISMONT for REC DOES arrangements. remembership of [?] Bipo Bank Amg.	
WATTEN	7.4.15	midnight	Marched from RECQUES to WATTEN - Fund camps tents and can commence re-pitching at once.	
"	8.4.15	"	Visited DDO Rent Army.	
"	9.4.15	"	Great quantity of stores arrived at Railhead ST OMER. Packed all day collecting.	
"	10.4.15	"	Another by consignment from Calais and some in a few hours to meet the unknown.	
"	11.4.15		O Corporate Brigade has been formed from the men left in the division. The brigade march today to XXIII Bupo in the RENINGHELST area. Visited Brigade at RENINGHELST to ascertain immediate requirements. Report sent not to meet an earlier tomorrow.	

WAR DIARY
or
INTELLIGENCE SUMMARY

(Erase heading not required.)

of CAPT D.R.SM. Army Form C. 2118
D A.D.O.S.
29 D.V.

Place	Date	Hour	Summary of Events and Information	Remarks and references to Appendices
WATTEN	1.4.18	N/m	Despatched long soft forward to advanced Corporate Brigade. Call to supply all other regiments. A Corporate Brigade has been formed. This Atelier has been moved to 101 Corpl Div. It has been equipped ready for being	
"	1.4.18	3pm	99th American Division is moving to this area and will be attached to the Division for training purposes. Visited B.O.R.	
"	2.4.18	10pm	Visited Ordnance Officer 99 American Division — He has very little knowledge of the supply of Ordnance Stores as would by British Army. The Quartermasters Dept. of the American Army supplies the greater part in America.	
"	3.4.18	11.30	Visited B.D.O. Calais — Arranged forwarding for supply to 99 Division. Infantry and M.G. units of the division are to be equipped at once on Initial Scale. Scale to be made out from Mobilization Store Table of Infantry, M.G. and Trench Mortar units. Arranged for a supply of H.Mk cartridges and a kitchen experiment to be sent off at once for next new armoury	

WAR DIARY of CAPT D.R SMITH

INTELLIGENCE SUMMARY D.A.D.O.S. 29 Div.

Army Form C. 2118

(Erase heading not required.)

Place	Date	Hour	Summary of Events and Information	Remarks and references to Appendices
WITTEN	17.4.18	11.0 a.m.	Rode over to Boulogne Brigade. Extremely hazy day organizing officer for 77 American Division.	
"	5.4.18	"	Lt. Col. Bentley has asked for refitting a great deal of Divn transport. Visited Bompard Bivouac and Calais –	
"	18.4.18	"	Investigated demand of 66 Div R.A. Instructions to one of two Batteries or one Park Horses and to collect three – 16.15.15 17 th Div.	
"	19.4.18	"	I know out to Calais to 66 R.A. Tpt Offr from American Div. has checked to tent wire rope – Have sent a D.O. to remain at American Headquarters – Orders despatched to Bompard Bde. 61 American Div.	
"	20.4.18	"	to hne lorries to Calais for 66 R.A. Divn. Transport busy handing over to American Div. D.O. out to check deficiencies	
"	21.4.18	"	Controls Rolls from 66 R.H. arrive to Second Rolls 77 & 50 under Hdqs 77 Div.	
"	22.4.18	"	1.20 Lewis Guns issued to American Div – Works are of this division	

WAR DIARY of CAPT D. R. SMITH
D.A.D.O.S. 39 D.V.

Army Form C. 2118.

Place	Date	Hour	Summary of Events and Information	Remarks and references to Appendices
WATTEN	23.4.18	6 pm	Visited 39 Division Ord. Instr. Workshops & Store to expte Repairing Repairs. Also Inspecting Personal Most Totals for Infantry of H.Q. unit.	229
"	24.4.18	6 pm	Visited work of American Repairs	229/
"	25.4.18	"		222/
"	26.4.18	"	Visited Hy. American Repairs and D.O.S. and D.D.O.S. Second Army.	223/
"	27.4.18 to 30.4.18		Visited various American Ord. Stores arranging for returning of	92/

J.R. Smith
D.A.D.O.S. 39 Dv.

WAR DIARY of CAPT D.R. SMITH — Army Form C. 2118.

INTELLIGENCE SUMMARY.
(Erase heading not required.)

D.A.D.O.S. 39 D.V.

Nov 25

Instructions regarding War Diaries and Intelligence Summaries are contained in F.S. Regs., Part II. and the Staff Manual respectively. Title pages will be prepared in manuscript.

Place	Date	Hour	Summary of Events and Information	Remarks and references to Appendices
WATTEN	1.5.18	6.30pm	Visited H.Q. 77 American Div. Introduced myself to commander 19.M. Aph [?]	
"	2.5.18	"	d.	
"	3.5.18	"	Visited Acme Army School of Sniping. Arranged for the renewal of Telescopic Sights that went with 77 Div.	
"	4.5.18	"	Compared Range taking — tried to complete equipments rec'd from Ordnance. Began to trace spare	
"	5.5.18	"	Visited Reserve Army to make arrangements for Supply Regts. U.S.A. not yet completed for supply Regt. of 77 Div. hot on Personnel	
"	6.5.18 to 13.5.18	"	Nothing of importance to relate. Visited units of 77 Div. and American Supply Officers on the matter of obtaining their stores.	
"		"	Returned a A.D.Off. Officer of 77 Div. a A.D.Off. of Ordnance Store in the field	
"	14.5.18	"	307/8 Regt. 77 Div. moved to Third Army. They were fully equipped	
"	15.5.18	"	Visited D.D.O.S. Third Army and Signed J.E. 307/8 Regt.	
"		"	Pro term.	
"	21.5.18	"	"	
"	22.5.18	"	30 American River has now arrived and is now proceeding to the Division. Visited Regt. 30 Div. & put into touch with D.O.O.	

Army Form C. 2118.

WAR DIARY
INTELLIGENCE SUMMARY.
(Erase heading not required.)

Instructions regarding War Diaries and Intelligence Summaries are contained in F. S. Regs., Part II. and the Staff Manual respectively. Title pages will be prepared in manuscript.

Place	Date	Hour	Summary of Events and Information	Remarks and references to Appendices
WATTEN	23.5.18	11 Am	Worked C.O.O. Camp out O.O. 30 American Div. Rale arrangement for	
	24.5.18		Appdx K 30 Div.	
	25.5.18		Visited 77 & 30 Divs.	
	26.5.18		"	
	27.5.18		Visited Ecles out O.O. 30 American Div. Col Ricknell Chief of 30 American Bri attending. Then long woman to the half at Eclen & enemy as instructed attacked the forward to the other train. Have put a R.O. in charge who will also of the referre and one Maj. are deputedted to the HQ of the referre unit	
	28.5.18		Visited until HQ of 30 American Bri. who arrived yesterday.	
	29.5.18		Visited and HQ of 30 American Bri. also 77 American Bri. Kabedg and Ordnance Reserves of both divisions.	
	30.5.18			

S.F. Mand. 64
D.A.D.O.S. 39 Div.

WAR DIARY
INTELLIGENCE SUMMARY.

Army Form C. 2118.

OF D.A.D.O.R. SMITH
D.A.D.O.S.
30 Division.

Place	Date	Hour	Summary of Events and Information	Remarks and references to Appendices
WATTEN	1.6.18	10.30pm	Visited 30 American Division	
"	2.6.18	"	Visited Ordnance Depôt Boulogne re taken on American personnel.	
"	3.6.18	"	Visited 30 & 77 American Divisions	
"	4.6.18	6.0	77th American army Park. They are to re-arm with American Rifle – Exchange to be carried out by. Approx 7,000 rifles arrives at Rickebrouck are here been sent out by Army to units here, to which to Bumps with British Rifles. Belgrade Lines MT Guns are also to be carried on.	S27 S26
"	5.6.18	"	All American Rifles chased by 1.0 pm the morning – lorries dispatched to Thurne army Park where for 30,000 Belgrade Rgd. 77 Div.	S25
"	6.6.18	"	Buy Rept. here returning with exchange rifle. Has arranged for all others to be Exhausted thro' my Dumps	S28
"	"	"	Approximately 16,000 Rifles now in Kit Dumps – lorries returning from 2nd & Army are with rifles.	S29
"	7.6.18	"	Visited 30 American Division	S30

Army Form C. 2118.

WAR DIARY
INTELLIGENCE SUMMARY.
(Erase heading not required.)

Place	Date	Hour	Summary of Events and Information	Remarks and references to Appendices
WATTEN	8.6.18	10 a.m	Visited 3 American Bns & units attached	APP
"	11.6.18	"	"	APP
"	"	"	5,600 Rifles, 800 Bayonets 170 Lewis Guns his taken over attacked by 77 Div. Orders ad Packhorse.	APP
"	12.6.18	"	Visited units of 30 American Division	APP
"	13.6.18	"	"	
"	14.6.18	"	Lunch 7.00 with G. Kuhn Comdg. 78 American Div. & the Division - Arranged for handover of 78 American Div. to the Division - Arranged to his personnel. Took O.C. 78 Div. Div. over 30 Div. Division arranging hing me to an establishing Sunl. offer at NIELLES LEZ BLEQUIN - Visited 30 American Division - Attended Conference at Divisional Headquarters - Branch officers established at NIELLES. To further moved 15 un from 30 Div. Command of American Rifles - 1500 Infantry	APP
"	15.6.18	"		APP

T. Barte

Army Form C. 2118.

WAR DIARY
INTELLIGENCE SUMMARY.
(Erase heading not required.)

Instructions regarding War Diaries and Intelligence Summaries are contained in F. S. Regs., Part II. and the Staff Manual respectively. Title pages will be prepared in manuscript.

Place	Date	Hour	Summary of Events and Information	Remarks and references to Appendices
WATTEN	24.1.18		Visited 78 American Division & 3 American Division	98/
"	25.1.18		d.	10/
"			Received instructions that we are to entrain for another American Division - viz 30th. Notes were sent round army	11/
"	26.6.18		Visited 78 Div. & DADVS 3rd Div. at SAMER and regime to	8/
"			taking on & to American Division -	
"	27.1.18		Established Head office at SAMER - A arrangement of	9/
"			30 th Division.	
"	28.6.18		Visited 30 th Division 75 R & 30 R Brig.	9/
"	29.6.18		d.	9/
"	30.1.18		d.	70/

Hammel Major
DADVS

14

WAR DIARY OI MAJOR R. SMITH Army Form C. 2118.
or
INTELLIGENCE SUMMARY. D.A.D.O.S. 29 Div
(Erase heading not required.)

Instructions regarding War Diaries and Intelligence Summaries are contained in F. S. Regs., Part II. and the Staff Manual respectively. Title pages will be prepared in manuscript.

Place	Date	Hour	Summary of Events and Information	Remarks and references to Appendices
WATTEN	17/6 to 4/7/18		Visited 3rd, 78th and 80th American Divisions. 30th American Division moved to WATOU area. Completed administration of Reinf. Btns - looked over details bns. and advised Lieut.s and Officers for OD 30th Div.	
	5/7/18 to 11/7/18		Normal routine. Visited American Divisions.	
			Visited 27th American Division. The Division is held up, Army regards administration. Td. American Army intends on to visit the O.O. and for but somehow regards trusting the staff of the Division. Had a conversation with average of British trusted in training the staff of the D.O.D. Left Cassel at 11 hours one of bodies on retired on Refulgation. Also Talk.	
	12/7/18 to 19/7/18		Visited American Divisions & concluded inclusion 27th & 30th American Divisions.	
	20/7/18		Left WATTEN for ENGLAND, a leave. RHSmith Major DADOS 29 Div	

Army Form C. 2118.

WAR DIARY OF MT&R
~~INTELLIGENCE~~ SUMMARY.
(Erase heading not required.)

D.R SMITH
S.M.T.O.C. 29 Div.

Instructions regarding War Diaries and Intelligence Summaries are contained in F. S. Regs., Part II. and the Staff Manual respectively. Title pages will be prepared in manuscript.

Place	Date	Hour	Summary of Events and Information	Remarks and references to Appendices
WATTEN	1.8.18–6.8.18		On leave to England.	/X/
"	7.8.18	10.30am	Visited R.D.D. Reve Army and A.S.D.T.S. Cy. Rofs.	/X/
"	8.8.18	"	Visited 30 K. and 27 K. American Divisions. First Shop are working quite satisfactorily.	/X/
"	9.8.18	"	Visited D.O.S. Second Army.	/X/
"	10.8.18	"	16 K.F.F. Bde Hy and 6 Cates Bkrs moved from First Army Troops. Visited Calais.	/X/
"	11.8.18	"	13 Rifle Bde, 16 Rifle Bde, 13 Rifle Cwm, 8/10 Gordon Highlanders, 7 Cameron Hylanders, 11 Argyll & Sutherland Highlanders being demobed – anyone for nephon of Armoured Battalions. Opened Imploying Range.	/X/
"	12.8.18	"	Visited Army Trofs.	/X/
"	13.8.18	"	First Imm, 39 Signal Coy, 50 Hy.Hd Vty Rect, 39 M.T. Coy. as Free Ambulance moved to D.O.K. Cy 66th Troops – to Calais Bkrs moved to 66 Division.	/X/
"	14.8.18	"	Instructions received to more of mem of Division from Second Army area to L.F.C.(S).
Moved 16 Bde & M.G.On. D631, 117 Bde & O.O. P00 W. 119 Bde to O.D. HAIRE	/X/

Instructions regarding War Diaries and Intelligence Summaries are contained in F. S. Regs., Part II. and the Staff Manual respectively. Title pages will be prepared in manuscript.

WAR DIARY ~~or INTELLIGENCE SUMMARY.~~ of Major D. R. Smith D.A.D.O.S. 39 Div.

(*Erase heading not required.*)

Army Form C. 2118.

Place	Date	Hour	Summary of Events and Information	Remarks and references to Appendices
WATTEN	1.8.18–6.8.18		On leave to England.	
"	7.8.18	10 pm	Visited D.D.O.S. Second Army and A.D.O.S. XV Corps.	
"	8.8.18	"	Visited 30th and 27th American Divisions. Find they are working quite satisfactorily.	
"	9.8.18		Visited D.D.O.S. Second Army	
"	10.8.18		116 Infy Bde Hdq and 6 Cadre Battns moved from First Army Troops. Visited Calais	
"	11.8.18		12 Royal Scots, 16 Royal Scots, 10 Royal [illegible] 8/10 Gordon Highlanders, 7 Cameron Highlanders, 11 Argyll & Sutherland Highlanders being disbanded. Arranged for reception of Stores at [illegible]. Opened temporary dump.	
	12.8.18		Visited Army & Corps	
	13.8.18		Div. Train, 39 Signal Coy, 50 Mobile Vety Sect, 39 M.T. Coy, 133 Field Ambulance moved to O.O. XV Corps Troops. 10 Cadre Battns ordered to 66 Division. Instructions received as to move of Division from Second Army area to L of C (S).	
	14.8.18		Moved 116 Bde to No 9 Ord. Depot, 117 Bde to O.O. ROUEN, 118 Bde to O.O. HAVRE	

D. D. & L., London, E.C. (A8001) Wt. W1771/M2031 750,000 5/17 Sch. 52 Forms C2118/14

WAR DIARY
or
INTELLIGENCE SUMMARY.
(Erase heading not required.)

Army Form C. 2118.

WO95/392 Vol 30

Place	Date	Hour	Summary of Events and Information	Remarks and references to Appendices
WATTEN	16.8.16	5 pm	4th E. Lancs and 1/7 H.L.R Balt] arrived from 4th Bo. Yorks. A.D.M.S. T. Gofton. Moved the following.	
DIEPPE	16.8.16			
VARENGE-VILLE	17.8.16		Fixed up lines camps. Yorks. D.D.M.S. L.J.C. (C)	
	18.8.16	6	normal routine	
	21.8.16		Yorks Regt. 1/5 Bde. and report to Offly of Coen to Training Camps.	
	22 & 23.8.16		normal routine	
	23.8.16		supplied Bde. H.Q. to 1/5 Bde.	
	24.8.16		Following units arrived from 50 Div and were reported on and 5, 6 and 8th Du Lyn to O.C. ROUEN. 4 and 5th Nor Hd Rds to O.C. HAVRE 4 and 5th Yorks Regt, and S. Staff and H.L.E Yorks to O.C. CALAIS	
	25.8.16		Bde W.O. despatched to 1/6 Bde.	
	26.8.16		normal routine	
	27.8.16			
	31.8.16			

Army Form C. 2118.

WAR DIARY
or
INTELLIGENCE SUMMARY.
(Erase heading not required.)

Instructions regarding War Diaries and Intelligence Summaries are contained in F. S. Regs., Part II. and the Staff Manual respectively. Title pages will be prepared in manuscript.

Place	Date	Hour	Summary of Events and Information	Remarks and references to Appendices
WATTEN	16th		4th E Kings and 1/7 K.R.R. Bttlf arrived from M. Stn. Variable	
			about 7 p.m.	
			Moved to billets.	
DIEPPE	17th			
			March to the camp. Worked hard. Topo 6.p.c. (6)	
VARENNE-PLAGE	18th			
	19th		Parade. notes.	
	21st			
	nightly		In the day in Bn. not report to Offr. I Coy to	
			Trainy Regt.	
	22nd		Whole minute.	
	23rd		Offr in the Bn. to Co. to Mr Bn.	
	24th		Following went away from so Bn. one sur asgne. and and	
			5 rank & file Royston to OO Rouen	
			4 same OM he Mk 7 M to OO Havre	
			4 nish Yorks Regt. M.S. Offr. and 4 h L E Yorks to OO CALAIS	
			Bn. WD despatched to WO Bde.	
	25th			
	26th			
			Albert Ally	
	27th		Route marches	
	28th			Brigadr 29 Bn.

Army Form C. 2118.

WAR DIARY 1/Major D.R.SMITH
or
INTELLIGENCE SUMMARY. D.A.D.O.S. 39 D10
(Erase heading not required.)

Place	Date	Hour	Summary of Events and Information	Remarks and references to Appendices
VARENGEVILLE	1.9.18 to 30.9.18		Nothing of importance to record.	

Bathwick Major
D.A.D.O.S. 39 Div.

31   39

Secret Confidential Army Form C. 2118.
of MAJOR D.R. SMITH
D.A.D.O.S. 36 DIV

WAR DIARY
or
INTELLIGENCE SUMMARY.
(Erase heading not required.)

Instructions regarding War Diaries and Intelligence
Summaries are contained in F. S. Regs., Part II.
and the Staff Manual respectively. Title pages
will be prepared in manuscript.

Place	Date	Hour	Summary of Events and Information	Remarks and references to Appendices
VARENGEVILLE	1.10.18 to 3.10.18		normal routine work.	
	4.10.18	9.30 a.m.	to Divisional Camp & king church at MARTIN EGLISE. Pour — ten entrances by B.G.G.S. & A.C. (S) & who was accompanying	
			for Divisional Review.	
	6.10.18	3 p.m.	visited D.D.V.S. & Martin Eglise.	
	6.10.18		Got G.O. & staff to Campion Rocket Project attention	
	7.10.18 to 16.10.18		normal motor work. Visited the Camp & have arranged the working of Veterinary Review	
	17.10.18		Dr Gare to PARIS	
	25.10.18 to 31.10.18		normal motor work.	Ellmiral Ruger DADOS 39 Div

Army Form C. 2118

WAR DIARY of D.A.D.O.S. 39 Div.
INTELLIGENCE SUMMARY
(Erase heading not required.)

Vol 33

Place	Date	Hour	Summary of Events and Information	Remarks and references to Appendices
MARANGEVILLE	1/10/18 to		Nothing unusual occurred.	Cert
"	24/10/18		Normal Routine without anything of importance to note.	Cert
"	25/10/18		No 2 L of C (B) Reception Camp administered for Gnl Services and personnel. Handed to MARTIN Louse Camp from C.O.O. Distr.	Cert
"	26/10/18		Visited Martin Louse Camp, everything OK.	Cert
"	27/10/18 to 30/10/18		Normal Routine without any notable happenings.	Cert

Wright Major
O/ADOS 39 Div.

WAR DIARY
or
INTELLIGENCE SUMMARY

Army Form C. 2118

troops 39 Div

Vol 34

Place	Date	Hour	Summary of Events and Information	Remarks and references to Appendices
VARENGEVILLE	1-12-18 to 31-12-18		Normal Routine took place nothing of special note happening	

Colonel
A.D.S.S.

31 DEC 1919 39th Division

Army Form C. 2118

WAR DIARY
or
INTELLIGENCE SUMMARY
(Erase heading not required.)

of S.A.A.D.5
29 Div

4/13

Place	Date	Hour	Summary of Events and Information	Remarks and references to Appendices
YARENGE VILLE	1-1-1919 to 31-1-1919		Normal Routine Work	

Capt Maj/n
h S.A.D.O.5

31 JAN 1919

Army Form C. 2118

WAR DIARY
or
INTELLIGENCE SUMMARY

(Erase heading not required.)

Instructions regarding War Diaries and Intelligence Summaries are contained in F.S. Regs., Part II. and the Staff Manual respectively. Title Pages will be prepared in manuscript.

of A.D.O.S of 29 Div

4/3

WO 95 /

Place	Date	Hour	Summary of Events and Information	Remarks and references to Appendices
VARENGEVILLE	1-2-19 to 28/2/19		Nothing of special note to record. Ordinary routine work	

Capt Major
for A.D.O.S.